Standing at the Crossroads

A Mentor's Inspirations

by Pastor Cory P. Pariseau and Pastor Jim Mullett

xulon
PRESS

Standing at the Crossroads
by Pastor Cory P. Pariseau and Jim Mullett

Printed in the United States of America

ISBN 9781619969810

www.xulonpress.com

Dedications

This book is dedicated to the following:

- My Lord and savior Jesus Christ, without whom none of this is possible
- My parents, Denny and Donna (Penny) Pariseau
- All my brothers, sisters, nieces and nephews - we are family!
- Pastor Jim Mullett and Family
- The Hillside Chapel Mennonite Church Congregational family
- Crossroads World Christian Center Church Partners, Families, and friends.
- Freelance writer and friend Sherrie Dennis
- Most of all, to my kids: Damian Zackary Marburger Pariseau,
- Isaiah Alexander Pariseau, and Suhanna Grace Pariseau.

I love you more than I can ever say. You have saved me from my self, and you showed me how to love beyond self. Remember, you can do anything and all things through Christ who will strengthen you.

Table of Contents

Forward

It came as a total surprise to me when I learned that a youthful friend had collected this material and compiled it into a manuscript intended for publication. I am indeed grateful to Cory for the work and expertise he has put into this project.

It has never been my intent to stand before the public eye, although I must confess it feels very good to leave behind this book as a legacy when I leave this world for the next. No rational person wants to go into oblivion and be forgotten.

Most of all I hope the reader understands that there is a God and Creator standing in the wings giving direction to His servant people who will listen and follow. It was not fate that brought my wife Isabel and me to Southern Ohio. It was none other than the plan of the Almighty.

All of this calls to mind my favorite hymn:

To God be the glory!
Great things he hath done!
So loved He this world
That He gave us his Son,

Who yielded Himself

An atonement for sin

And opened the life-gates

That all may go in.

Praise the Lord!

Hey, and I sing a great tenor whenever that song is announced!

– Pastor Jim

Section I:

My Story – by Pastor Cory P. Pariseau

Introduction

"Stand at the crossroads and look; ask for the ancient paths,
ask where the good way is, and walk in it,
and you will find rest for your souls."
– Jeremiah 6:16

A story has to begin somewhere. Not for sure why this one begins with me. Actually, this story begins far beyond and outside of me, as all stories truly begin.

I could technically say all stories begin in the book of Genesis. If you want to go that far back, I warmly invite you to come to church! In the meantime, consider this story to be my chapter in the book of spiritual journeys.

I'm starting the story here, because in order for you to fully understand the passion I have for my mentor's inspirational notes, I feel you need to see what I went through as the person reading them.

In the hills of southeast Ohio, in the hollows of Jackson County, sits a picturesque church called Hillside Chapel Mennonite Church.

Many of the sweetest moments of my upbringing were within these walls.

Looking back now, the wise and encouraging words of my childhood pastor still ring in my ears. So profoundly was I affected by the love and guidance here that I was inspired to become a pastor myself.

Serving a loving and all-powerful God every Saturday evening, Pastor Jim Mullett would speak words of wisdom from his beautiful heart - the heart of a man who serves his congregation still, even during "retirement."

You see, pastoring is like the unwritten street gang law: 'Once you're in, you're in for life.' You can say you quit, but people will always be drawn to you for help. Something stays on you as a pastor.

My memories are vivid and powerful. It makes me wonder how I ever made it through to this day. Knowing God is the Author and Finisher of my life and that everything has a purpose and a reason, I choose to believe that God is using what I went through to help change people's lives in the inner-city of Columbus, Ohio and around the world.

How did I get to this point? How did I even survive my early childhood? How did I make it from the deadly streets of Newark, Ohio to become a pastor? Well, let me tell you.

I was blessed.

I believe I would not be in this position to help others if God did not put people in my life who did the same for me. In my school life, there were the nuns at St. Peter and Paul's school, and my 11th and 12th grade teacher Mrs. Diana Lintla.

Since beginning to raise a family, being the single father of three kids, I've needed all the help I could get - and God made sure I got it. There's Louis Comair who has been a huge blessing. And then there are all the great people I got to meet throughout the years at Parents Anonymous Inc., a parent support group which helps prevent child abuse.

God placed so many people in my life to make a difference, or to put me back on the right road to where He could use me. But I feel I owe the most to the miraculous family that took me in, and the Pastor who helped guide me spiritually.

I grew up on a farm in southeastern Ohio on the outskirts of a small town called Wellston. My adoptive family, the Pariseaus, consisted of Mom (Donna) and Dad (Dennis) myself, and 17 other kids of different races, backgrounds and ages. This created a satire in Jackson County, but when Dennis and Donna Pariseau adopted us, they took all of our disjointed and troubled pasts and made us a family.

The Pariseaus provided a sanctuary for me to recover from all the sexual, physical and mental abuse I endured as a child. Mom instinctively seemed to be guided to say and do the right things to get me through it.

Mom gave us the foundation in church and provided us the opportunity for education in a Christian school. Dad gave us his work ethic and skills to go out, work hard and make a living. Parenting, I've learned, is not easy. They did the best they could and shared with us all that God had given them. And Pastor Jim helped me to see God's hand in all of it.

The road to that beautiful farm and family was long and treacherous. To put it mildly, my childhood was very difficult. Let's just say I have no fear of Hell. I've already been there.

Chapter One

When I Was a Child

"When I was a child, I spake as a child,
I understood as a child, I thought as a child…"
– 1 Corinthians 13:11

I was born Cory Eugene Bates in Erie, Pennsylvania, July 20, 1969 - the very same day when mankind landed on the moon ("one small step for man, one giant leap for mankind").

My biological mother Janet was a beautiful African American woman small in stature, but big in might. Men loved her, and women hated her. My biological father Ernie was a handsome man, tall and mixed with Sioux and African American. It was the same with him. He made women swoon, and men wanted to kill him.

My mother already had four other children when she met my father. Even so, he took to her beauty and charm right away. She, like practically every woman in his path, fell for him as well.

Like a stiff mixed drink, this marriage of strong brews created swirls of sweet in a mostly bitter pool, and was perpetually on the rocks.

I was child number five. Eventually, there were seven of us. Three girls, four boys. Annette, Lynette, Janetha, J.B. Ernest, Martin, and me.

I remember many things from the time when I was still in diapers. The east side of Newark, Ohio. Back in the day they used to call it little Chicago. Real gangs, drugs running rampant, prostitution and bars lined up side by side.

I remember the apartment above the bar we lived in and the house we later moved to, out front of the railroad tracks. I remember the after-parties my parents used to have when they came home from the bar. I would toddle around after the crowd dispersed, picking up discarded beer cans, claiming the last sips of golden grown-up juice from each. Sometimes I would get the ash can, receiving an unexpected swig of cigarette-butt juice. YUCK!

I look back now, knowing I was still in diapers but able to walk and get around. "Cory Eugene Bates! What are you doing out of bed?" my mom would yell at me. Then she'd kiss me and swat me on the butt, push me back into my room and put me to bed.

There were even times when things seemed to be "normal." Mom and Dad would come home for a bit, there would actually be food in the house, but it never lasted long. As the turmoil took over the atmosphere of my biological family home, the flavor of our family became less and less golden juice and ever more frequent sips from the ash can. The bitterness of that swill started to take hold. Fights, screaming, arguments.

It was during these emotional pyrotechnics that our oldest brother, J.B., became the man of the house at the age of nine. My oldest sister, Annette, became the woman of the house. Both were streetwise and smart, and both took after my biological mother - small in stature but mighty in strength. They took care of us kids the best they could.

Chapter Two

The Big Argument

"And the contention was so sharp between them, that they departed asunder one from the other..."
–Acts 15:39

Arguments happen. Everyone argues. My brother Ernest and I fought like cats and dogs. But we loved each other at the same time. In other words, we were typical brothers.

It brings to mind a time when we were having a big fight. Mom came in and put a stop to it. She made us hug each other for a long time. Then she made us kiss each other in front of everyone in the house. They all laughed and laughed at us. Even though we didn't always get along, we siblings really did have a lot of love for each other. Ernest and J.B. still watch over me even now.

But some arguments are worse than others. Some spiral totally out of control. One thing leads to another, and the next thing you know, there's deep trouble. One horrible argument changed everything forever. Even J.B and Annette couldn't save the day.

The memories are sharp and disjointed by trauma. Noise outside. Shouting. I woke up from my nap. More shouting. It was a huge fight. I went out to the porch and steadied myself on the wooden post. Mom and Dad were going at it.

My mom was in a rage. Nothing could stop her. She had a knife in her hand, and she was chasing my dad around a vacant lot. The whole neighborhood came out to see what was going on, and all I could do is stand on the porch and cry.

"Get those kids back in the house!" someone said. "They don't need to see this!" I clung to the wooden post, helpless. I watched my parents run around and around until my mother finally caught up with Dad and stabbed him. They stopped and my father fell to the ground with the knife in is belly. My mother, realizing what she'd done, fell over him sobbing.

After that event things went South. Child Protective Services came into the picture. Mom had to go away for a little while. Whether it was prison, rehab or a mental facility, I don't know. I remember lying on Dad's chest when he got out of the hospital. I ran my fingers over the stab wound.

"Is this where mom hurt you?" I asked.

"Yes."

"I hate her for hurting you."

Dad picked me up and shook me. "Boy, don't you *ever* say that! She is your *mother*!" Then, just as quickly as the anger came, it subsided and turned to remorse. He gently laid me back on his chest.

Not long after, I remember him making all us kids clean the house because Mom was coming back home. We did a beautiful job scrubbing the carpets and the floors and the walls.

Then the big day came. I remember Mom coming home with two brown bags of groceries saying, “anybody hungry?” Mom was back, Dad was healing, the house was clean, and there was food. Things were looking up.

But once darkness gets a hold on people, it doesn’t give up so easily. The fighting began again. Then the escapism with drugs, alcohol and wild parties. No food in the house. Constant gnawing hunger. Getting sexually assaulted by the babysitter. The darkness came back to the house, and this time, it was here to stay.

Of all the things I went through, one of the memories that hits me the hardest was seeing my biological mother for the last time. The situation simply wasn’t fit for children, and we all found ourselves in court. Things went badly.

As CPS representatives took me away from the court house that night my mother bent down and held me. She told me she would be a way for a while, but she would come back for me. I knew she loved us, and I wanted to believe her words. But something in my gut told me I would never see her again.

After that we spent the night sleeping on top of the desks at the CPS office until morning when other beds could be found. It was too late in the day to contact potential fosters or to find open beds at the children’s home.

We didn't know what would happen to us. The next morning the CPS agents were scrambling, hard at work trying to place all seven of us. One by one each kid got a place. The last placement was me and my brother Ernest with a family on the other side of town. I don't know exact relationship with our family. Whether they simply knew us or were relatives, they were good people all the same. But we couldn't stay there permanently. Thus began the foster-go-round.

Chapter Three

Can't Forget

"Then thou scarest me with dreams,
and terrifiest me through visions..."
– Job 7:14

We got bounced through the foster care system like a ball in a pinball machine. There were some good foster parents, and then there were some in it for the money. Some families were downright criminal, and some loved us, but were unable to handle us and our emotional issues.

Going in and out of the foster homes kept me totally off balance. Back then, no one really understood learning disabilities, so I could not read or write. Jeered for having a hard time with book learning, shoved around from one place to another, and receiving a confusing intermittent mixture of love and abuse, I lost the ability to trust by the age of seven.

We did have one steady, recurring theme in our scattered lives. Cindy and Judy. Once in a while throughout all of this, these two women would come to check up on us.

I still don't know exactly who these lovely souls were. Something about them was very reassuring. They took an interest in our family very early on. I knew their names, and I knew they were kind, and I knew they were very beautiful. I would marvel at Judy's long, long, black hair.

Everything else was a mystery. I don't know what agency they were with, if any. Were they sent, or did they visit because they wanted to? Maybe they were angels in disguise. Who knows?

They kind of reminded me of Laverne and Shirley, in a 'stick together, and we can make it' kind of way. Whenever they visited they always gave me a good feeling. Like we had someone in our corner, even though everything was in constant turmoil.

In all, there were at least two children's homes, and a dozen or so foster homes. Each children's home and foster home also had its own adventure. Some of them had horror stories. There was one in particular, Ms. McCarty, who lived in the Twilight Zone.

I remember on arriving that in my mind, the house seemed to loom overhead like a movie mansion. In reality it was a rancher with a garage and gravel driveway. When you're small and in a strange place, everything seems intimidating.

To this day, I don't know if she was taking in children to truly foster them, or to be able to display to her community what a good citizen she was for saving lost children. It really is hard to tell. I'm sure she meant well on some level, but she found the weirdest possible ways to show it.

The house was kind of like a revolving door for foster kids. There was Ernest and me, and for a short time there was Martin and my little sister Lynette. Later, Martin and Lynette were placed elsewhere. Then there were Mike and Susan, and Nicole, and Heather.

We all became kind of like a support group subculture for each other just to get through the bizarreness. Kind of like Ms. McCarty's Kids Anonymous. We had a special connection, and though we've grown apart over the years, we're family for life.

Ms. McCarty would do strange things like go out and buy herself sweets and wonderful food and hoard them while making us all eat cabbage soup every single day. It was hard living. A roof, a bed, meager food, but not one single hug.

I'm reminded of Proverbs 15:17: "Better [is] a small serving of herbs with love, than a stalled ox with hatred therewith." I don't think Ms. McCarty hated us. Some people simply don't have a frame of reference for affection. We felt tolerated, but never loved. The cabbage soup would have been fine, if only there was love to go with it.

Then there was the time when she dropped me off outside the house from daycare and went out somewhere with the other kids. I can't remember if she forgot to let me in the house, if she forgot to pile me in the car, or if she deliberately left me out of the house. What I do remember is standing outside in the frozen dead of winter for hours.

By the time they all got back, I was shivering uncontrollably and feeling ill. She told me I had frostbite. Then, and keep in mind this is just one example of life in the Twilight Zone, somehow it made sense to her to cover me with snow in the bathtub. All it did was make me wet as well as cold, and sicker.

Even at my young age, I knew Ms. McCarty wasn't quite right, and so did everyone else. Things got weirder and worse. It got to the point that one day I sneaked in a phone call for help. I didn't know who to dial, so I just talked to the operator and told her to send someone to get us all out of there.

It worked. We did get out of there. We found sweet relief when we were placed in a New Age village for foster children in Goshen, Ohio. Goshen. Looking back, Goshen is the perfect name for the condition we were all in. The village in Goshen was a place where we could be shielded and catch our breath while the plagues of Egypt raged in the world outside.

It was a foster home meets children's home type of atmosphere. Imagine a housing community where families came to live just to take care of foster kids lost in the system. I remember this short time fondly. I still like the idea and concept of the village because it really does take a village to raise kids.

We stayed in different houses. My brother J.B. and I were in one, and my brothers Ernest, Martin, and my sister Lynette were in another. We were spread out but still together, trying to heal in emotional convalescence.

Chapter Four

The Visitor

"A time to laugh...a time to dance..." – *Ecclesiastes 3:4*

Even though the burden of our combined emotional baggage was spread out, it was still heavy. We needed some kind of diversion. We needed something we hadn't had in a long time: fun.

And who should show up right on time? Judy! It felt like ages since we saw her and Cindy last. Judy was the most beautiful woman I had ever seen. Even after a long time between visits, her smile could still melt my little heart, and her hair was still spectacular.

Judy wasn't the only one who could melt hearts. I have to say, I had major cuteness as a child, and I could work it. Remember Arnold on Different Strokes and Webster? I was both rolled up into one. Cory Arnold Webster Bates.

As they say, you can catch more flies with honey than you can with vinegar. Why anyone would want to catch flies, I don't know. But you get the idea. Even though I hated getting my cheeks pinched, I used my adorable status to my advantage. I knew a good thing when I had it, and whenever Cindy and Judy would visit, I turned on the charm.

I remember being at the visitation center and giving Judy the biggest hug. She and Cindy were bright spots in our lives, and I knew they had love for us, whoever they were.

I looked around for Cindy, but I didn't see her anywhere. I did the puppy dog eyes and said, "where's Cindy?"

"She's away, but she told me to tell you she said hi, and she misses you very much," said Judy. I sulked a little. But just one of them was enough to light up a room, so I was okay with just seeing Judy.

We all sat around together, talking about things. Judy listened with care and concern. Then she said that she had a surprise for us. She told us that she was going to take us all camping the next week!

We were all so excited we thought we would burst. We couldn't wait to go camping. The idea was like a fantasy. Camping was something we had never done before.

That week took forever. A week seems like a year to a little boy, but one day at a time, the week crept ever closer, and the anticipation grew and grew. The day finally came, and I made sure I was packed well in advance.

Lovely Judy picked us all up at the visitation center and we all piled ourselves and our stuff into the car. The scenic roads wound around the countryside like an asphalt river carrying us to paradise. The trip was an hour and forty-five minutes to beautiful Rio Grande, Ohio.

Chapter Five

I Found a Penny

"Ask, and it shall be given you; seek, and ye shall find..."
– Matthew 7:7

When we got to the campground, we were spellbound. We had never seen so many trees in one place. This was the first of many trips here.

As a child, I remember the trees and how beautiful it was. In retrospect, I look back now on the campground, and I realize now that the campground was a place of healing. We would gather at this place with other foster kids. And bit by little bit, we would recover from the traumas and nightmares.

Here among the trees and nature, we could really feel the peace we were looking for. Here, everything seemed possible. At this camp, a happy and bright future for my siblings and me didn't seem so far away.

I didn't know it at the time, but the Camp was called ACT which stands for Adopt a Child Today. All I knew was that it was an amazing place, and I was having fun with Judy and my brothers and all the other kids at the camp. Unbeknownst to any of us, Judy had a plan to find us a new family where my siblings and I all live together.

My first impression of this place and the experience is still vivid. When we arrived, I saw happy kids running around everywhere. Kids of all different colors, ages and backgrounds. Some were deaf, some were in wheelchairs. Everyone was different, but no one was unhappy.

So off we went. Making friends was easy here. It was amazing to see everyone getting along. J.B. quickly became the most popular kid at the camp, getting chummy with three boys from a family that arrived in a big brown bus. Boys with biblical names. Matthew, Mark and John.

Two apostles and a disciple. I wondered how many other apostles were on the bus. Andrew! There we go! Ernest and I got our very own apostle! We hung around Andrew. All kidding aside, they were a really cool family. We really hit it off.

All this socializing made me hungry, so I went in search of food. I went into the camp kitchen and saw some Ho Hos – the food of champions! I summoned my cuteness, and I asked the person there if I could have a Ho Ho with a long, drawn-out "pleeeaase" at the end of the sentence. They smiled and told me to look for a penny.

I really wanted that Ho Ho, so I went all over the camp asking one person after another, "excuse me, but they said I have to ask for a penny to get a Ho Ho." I was getting hungrier and hungrier.

Just when I was about to give up, a young woman came up to me. She seemed very much in charge. She could see I was exhausted from walking all over the camp asking for a penny. I hadn't asked her yet. Just as I was about to, she said, "my name is Penny. Were you asking for me?"

Oops. The person in the camp kitchen told me to ask for *Penny*, not *a* penny. "I was asking for a penny to buy a Ho Ho because I'm hungry," I said. Penny had the eye twinkle of suppressed laughter.

"Come with me," she said. She took me by the hand, and got one of the older boys in her family to go and reach for the box of Ho Hos since she was small. Small in stature, mind you. I would find out later throughout my life that dynamite comes in small packages, as they say.

This was Penny Pariseau, the family matriarch with the big brown bus. Matthew, Mark, John and Andrew were all with the Pariseaus as well. Penny handed me a Ho Ho and said, "what do you say, Cory?"

I said, "thank you, Penny." I haven't forgotten my manners since. To this day, I still make sure I say things like 'please, thank you, you're welcome, yes, sir,' etc. And I made sure to bring up my children the same way. Respect is a reciprocal thing.

Learning to be mannerly paid off. Two weeks after leaving the camp after the Ho Ho adventure, Judy came to visit. She smiled and said, "Penny was very impressed with you, Cory. She wants to know if you'd like to be a part of their family."

I didn't know what to think. I liked every Pariseau I'd met so far, but I also grew up thinking that good things never last. I wanted to be around my new friends from camp again, but the idea of living with them seemed surreal somehow.

Later on, my siblings and I all went back to the visitation center to meet the Pariseaus again. As they came out of that big brown bus of theirs, in my mind they looked like the Partridge Family.

We all went to the gymnasium to sit around and talk around the table there. They said that they had all taken a vote and decided that they wanted all of us to join the Pariseau family.

With a lifetime of troubles, it was hard to trust, but somehow, for the first time in a long time, I felt hope. The next week Denny Pariseau came down in a station wagon and picked us up. Two weeks before Christmas, it was the best present ever.

Chapter Six

Meeting Pastor Jim

"Train up a child in the way he should go...
he will not depart from it."
– Proverbs 22:6

The Pariseaus were (and still are) a special group of people. We felt liked we belonged right away. Denny and Donna Pariseau are the two most loving and caring people I know in my life. They took a lot of hardship upon them adopting me and my brothers.

I can't give them just page or two. It wouldn't do them justice. It has to be a book. I want to title it *Gods Family*. I think you will understand the title of the next book once you start reading it. But let me finish this one first.

It took some adjusting to settle into living out in the country. Many things were new to me. Time moved differently on the farm. Morning always came sooner than I wanted it to.

Things have to get done on farms, and you have to start very early. So we did. We would get up with the sun and do the chores.

Even though I knew things needed to get done, I did *not* like getting up early *at all.*

Not all the chores were in the early morning, and not all of them were dull. I remember waiting for the mailman to come. I used to think it was funny how he would drive his little truck from the wrong seat.

As soon as I knew he was nearby, I would try to beat him to the mailbox before he put the envelopes in. Some kids play video games. But this was the country. When you live on a farm, you play *Race the Mailman.*

Farm life was different, but wonderful. There were chores, love, and church. Church was a very important part of life. We would put on our best clothing. Nothing outrageous, but neat, clean and pressed. We weren't fancy, but we were always presentable.

I remember my first day at church with the Pariseaus. We made our way to the church. I was a little nervous. I was told I was going to get to meet the pastor. I wondered what he'd think of me.

We arrived at the little white building to see people smiling, chatting, shaking hands. I saw a familiar looking man. Then it dawned on me. It was the mailman. I didn't recognize him right away in his church clothes.

My family walked up to the mailman to say hello. When they greeted the mailman with, 'good morning, Pastor,' I was completely confused. I looked at him in disbelief. He was tall, so he bent down to greet me personally.

"How are you doing, young man?"

"You can't be the pastor," I said. He grinned.

"Why not?"

"Because you're the mailman!" He stood up and laughed.

"Yes," he said, "I am also the mailman."

This was Pastor Jim Mullett. Humble in nature, tall, and very eager to teach the word of God. He could boast that he had one of the first mixed race congregations in Jackson County. And with the Pariseaus, he could boast that the largest single family in Jackson County was attending his sermons.

But he would not. Boasting wasn't his style. He was more concerned with the spiritual welfare of the people in his church than having any claim to fame. The only praise he sought was praise of the Almighty.

I went into the sanctuary after everyone left and stood there alone. No one else was there, just me and God. I felt something, a connection that would bind me for a life time. Even though I was only 7 years old I knew God was up to something, and I would never be the same.

God has funny ways of doing things. I'm all grown up now and a pastor myself. Looking back, Pastor Jim Mullett, his family and the Congregation of Hillside Chapel left a mark on my heart that can never be erased.

We are made in God's image. Having had the opportunity and blessing to be in the good company of Pastor Jim and the Pariseaus, I have seen the proof.

My prayer is that you can find comfort in the words and wisdom of a man who has truly has a pastor's heart and love for the word of God and passionate heart for Gods people.

Section II:

Jim's Story – by Pastor Jim Mullett

Chapter Seven

Jim's Story

Isabel. The first time I seen her I knew she was special. *God help me* was my prayer. So after walking several rounds through the school library and her sister finally telling her to stop, I breathlessly caught up and ask her for a date. My prayer was answered!

Mother breathed a sigh of relief when I married that angelic young lady, Isabel. Perhaps there was a ray of hope for her son after all.

I grew up a rebel in a very sheltered and conservative church in which there were some folks who considered themselves better than me but were hiding their own sins. However there were people who I knew were sincere in their prayers and support of me as a young teenager finding his way.

One of them was my dad who wisely knew that rules would not contain me. Many nights after farm chores were finished and the lights in the barn were out, Dad would not be coming in. I would slip out to check on him and would hear him inside kneeling at a bale of hay praying for his son.

Were it not for these three people, my mother, father and dear Lucy, this book would not be written. Who knows what I would have become without these lanterns on the dark path?

When I was courting Isabel, Vietnam was just beginning to gain attention here in America. But somewhere deep within my soul I knew that killing and fighting was not the way to true peace, even in the military.

Just before marriage I went to my draft board and volunteered as a conscientious objector. The smile left the lady's face. She looked at me as though I were an errant child. "Oh," she said, "you're one of *those*." Her disdain didn't change my mind one bit. I was assigned to do two years of medical service in a hospital in Cincinnati as a civilian, and that was fine with me.

Very soon thereafter, Isabel and I connected with a small downtown church at the foot of Sycamore Hill. I also enrolled in night classes and became a certified automatic transmission technician. After I was released by Selective Service, Pastor Chuck asked if perhaps we would be interested in Christian Service.

Our denomination had just built a new mission church in Jackson County and needed persons to relate to youth. We soon discovered that Jackson was the last place in Ohio where you would go to look for a job. In 1963 there weren't any.

So we told the bishop we would go - *if God could provide employment.* A later weekend Bishop Menno was traveling through Columbus and by chance stopped for a bite to eat. At the same time a businessman named Joe from Wellston also stopped at the same restaurant. The two were acquainted and had a conversation. Joe said he would see what he could do as to finding employment for us.

Joe returned to his desk the following Monday and forgot all about his promise until Friday afternoon he suddenly remembered. Right away, he picked up the phone and dialed a local car dealership. When the owner answered and heard the request, there was a pause and then a small laugh.

"It's rather strange that you should call at this particular time," he said. "You see, my service manager just walked into my office. He is sitting here now asking where we might find a transmission mechanic!"

So we moved to Jackson County knowing without a doubt this was where God wanted us. We had no thought that we would spend the remainder of our life at that little church!

Our daughter, Wanda Sue, was six months old when we came to Jackson County. Two years later our first son, Wendell, was born. But to our horror, he was born with a rare and deadly blood disorder. He only lived for three months, and he was laid to rest in the church cemetery.

We may have lost our beloved Wendell, but God saw fit to do for us what he did for faithful Job by blessing us with another son,

Douglas. We were overjoyed! We had a second son to tide us over until that day when we'll all be reunited with our Wendell in God's care. After little Doug was born, we considered our family complete.

Time brought more changes into our lives. I became pastor of our church when the senior retired. Having dropped out of high school in my junior year I enrolled in adult basic education and passed the GED test with flying colors. I was on a roll! I got a real taste for learning, so I took some more college courses.

School felt great, and I was happy to learn. But I was also happy to earn! So, on a whim I took the postal entrance exam. Six months later, an opening appeared, and I was offered a position. We were grateful. Keeping a family of four fed was no easy task, even back then.

About this time our children were in grade school, and it was through school that we had the good fortune to meet the Pariseau family. Our children became fast friends and often visited each other after school and at church functions.

One of my favorite memories of getting to know the Pariseau children was an evening at the supper table. The main dish was a large bowl of chicken and noodles. I helped myself to a modest portion knowing there would be seconds and more. The bowl stopped by Cory's brother who was the youngest and smallest person to be served.

"Oh," he said, "chicken and noodles is my favorite!" He paused to look around and make sure each plate was served then nonchalantly dumped the entire remaining contents from the bowl on his plate. Without further comment he ate the whole thing!

The book project has been a delightful excuse to reminisce about this dear family. Denny and Donna (Penny, as we knew her) Pariseau adopted twelve children, and then she became pregnant and had two more. Denny had a cleaning business and had plenty of help from the family.

As the kids matured into adulthood, they one by one left home to pursue a life of their own. Some went to college, others went to find employment. Most of them moved away from Jackson to places like Portsmouth and California, Wilmington, Columbus, Newark, Cleveland, and Wheeling.

Oh how empty and lonely the nest became. The big house on the hill was now far too large. Denny having fulfilled his calling, having fought a good fight and finished the course passed away at too young an age.

Penny was now a free person and enrolled at Ohio State University for her master's degree and to pursue a profession in social counseling. Her career was cut short by a massive stroke that left her totally paralyzed.

It was a bitter/sweet reunion that brought the family back together in the hospital. In the ICU she could not put her thoughts into words, but she desperately wanted me to understand her request. She wanted the Sacraments. So we arranged a communion service the next day.

After an extended stay in the hospital, Penny moved into a nursing home in Wellston, determined to regain the use of her arms and hands. Her mind was sharp, and she regained speech, but nothing else worked. So she laid for over a year until finally she had enough movement in the right arm to control a scooter chair. Now she was again mobile! And with her lap top computer she was in touch with the world.

She got very good at maneuvering her chair. On one beautiful summer afternoon she slipped away from the confines of the home and drove her chair uptown, finding several yard sales. She had the time of her life! Oh, that was against the rules, but a real triumph for our hero!

Even with her disability Penny was the life of the party. She never complained and happily went to her reward in Heaven.

After I retired I began to write short inspirational messages that I would send out online each Sunday morning. Didn't God promise somewhere in the Bible that if we cast our bread upon the water after many days it would return? For me, the Internet was still somewhat of a new concept. I had no idea how far or where those short messages would go.

I wrote about personal and family experiences. I wrote about the words of Jesus. I wrote about life in America and the hills of Ohio. I wrote from a deep desire for peace, both national and personal.

I began to receive feedback, most of which was positive. There were however several who became angry when I refused to get on their soapbox and support their personal ideals and agendas.

There have been many responses to my weekly e-mails over the years, but none of them were in book form – until now. When I left my childhood spiritual community to go to Bible school in Canada, little did I know that in years to come my path would cross with a little black boy who was destined to fulfill God's purpose in Columbus, Ohio.

I never saw this book coming. But when God has something in mind, we seldom see it coming, do we?

Section III:

Inspirations from Pastor Jim

A Collection of Messages from Pastor Jim

Confronting Our Fears

The ancient mariners feared the uncharted waters too far from shore. Their nautical maps noted; beyond, there be dragons and they drew pictures of fire breathing monsters. When God spoke to Job He painted a picture of this mythical creature and called it Leviathan. Our Nation's fears and my fears are evident in the presidential debates of the past weeks. As a people our confidence is in our mighty Military machine fueled by the Religious Right. We run this machine arrogantly and roughshod into and over other Nations and then we wonder why they hate us so. Ron Paul of Texas understands this problem and dares to speak out but none of the other candidates want to hear. As Christians our confidence has been misplaced. God can and will be in control if we as a Nation choose to follow the teachings of Jesus in the Sermon on the Mount. It is the only way to lasting peace. Leviathan represents our fears. I give you God's promise in Isaiah 27: 1 **In that day the Lord with His severe sword, great and strong, will punish Leviathan the fleeing Serpent. He will slay the Reptile that is in the sea.** History teaches us that Military Power will fail. Faith in God must be our strength. Think about it…..Jim

In the Quiet Moments

He was just a small dog but this dog was special. He was the same age as our youngest grandchild and lived in the same family for sixteen years. Old age takes its toll even on our pets and so this week he was lovingly laid to rest under the plum tree. It was a long and tough decision to finally take him on that last trip to the vet. Grief and sadness is a part of life that overtakes us and nothing we can do will stop it. In the quiet moments we shed our tears. Tears are therapeutic, provided for us by a loving God. Jesus, as an adult male wept at the tomb of His dear friend Lazarus. He feels our pain and promised never to leave us. It's comforting to know He will walk with us while time brings healing and joy returns. Rest easy little Jingles. We love you…..Jim

The Ceremony

Boats, Weddings and beauty; Jesus enjoyed them all. Yes Isabel and I are in Canada. This evening we attended a beautiful wedding on board a boat on Lake Ontario. The ceremony, the meal, the reception stretched the imagination making a most memorable experience with the city of Toronto in the back-round. The Chinese bride and Canadian groom made a lovely couple. May God bless the union with long life and happiness. In our culture and society today marriages that last a lifetime are becoming the exception but Jesus can make it happen. In John's gospel chapter two Jesus preformed His first miracle at a wedding. Verse 11 says **He manifested His Glory.** It is His love that shines on us and we reflect it back to Him. So it is in marriage as husbands and wives reflect each-others love. Love is not only a romantic feeling but a commitment to always enhance the life of my mate both spiritually as well as physically. It is to be the best that I can be and give my best to my partner. After all, Jesus gives us His divine life just because he loves us. He is our model in marriage. Whether you are single or married love is a wonderful experience. Try it; you'll like it...Jim Mullett

Mother's Day

Mother's Day! Some were good, some were bad, and most were in-between. Consider the widow of Zarephath in 1 Kings 17: There was a severe famine, she was gathering firewood to bake the last bit of food for her and a son and then expected to die. She gave it to a man of God trusting the words of Elijah that the oil and flour would outlast the famine. She was a woman of great faith yet in verse 18 she alludes to a sinful life. She was an ordinary mother whose life was touched by the Grace of God in her hour of need.

How about us today, with the fuel gauge on empty and gas at $3.19 per gallon we can depend on God to sustain us. Good Mothers can always find a miracle when times get tough…Jim Mullett

Irregular People

Irregular People! Some folks just don't fit in with our normal understanding of how life should be. They march to a different drum all by themselves and consider the rest of the world to be out of step. In our communities, in our churches and in our families, the closer they are to us the more we become frustrated with their thoughts and actions. We can spend our lifetime trying to change them to no avail. What can one do when we reach the end of our rope except hang on and pray that it don't end in a rampage as it did in Virginia? Jesus in the Beatitudes said: **Blessed are those who mourn for they shall be comforted.** OK so none of my irregular people shot anyone yet, but Jesus could you hurry up a bit with the comfort??? Jim Mullett

By Faith

Oh those people of Faith in Hebrews 11! Abel, Enoch, Noah, Abraham, Sarah, Isaac, Jacob, Joseph and Moses, Even the harlot Rahab and the list goes on. What about us today? We too are people of Faith. Verse three says **By faith we understand that the worlds were framed by the Word of God**. And thank God for verse 40: **God having provided something better for us that they should not be made perfect apart from us.** But then I would never measure up to Abraham or Moses. I'm with the guy that prayed Lord I believe, help my unbelief. For ordinary people like you and me there is only the free gift of God's Grace. I accept it by faith......Jim

The Final Book

Resurrection Morning! Jesus is the undisputed King of Kings and Lord of Lords and He says to us; **I bestow upon you a kingdom just as My Father bestowed one upon Me that you may eat and drink at My table in My Kingdom.** Luke 22: 29 & 30. Is this our reward for being servants of God or is it a gift of His love and Grace? I think it's both. The final book of the bible is a Revelation of Jesus Christ and He shall reign forever and ever. The evil Devil has been defeated and will be cast into a lake of fire never to return again. Our God is alive! ...Jim

Could This Be Real?

Could this be real? The bible says in **Hebrews 13: 2 Some have unwittingly entertained angels.** Thursday evening, April 5, Isabel, our grandson Tyler and I were traveling North on interstate 75 in

Southern Georgia on our way home from Florida. We had spent the previous night and most of that day in a motel while our car was being repaired. Now the problem re-occurred and we were stranded along the hi-way in a remote area. The sun was low in the sky. Tyler and I were out of the car. I had raised the hood and was looking at the engine. When I turned around there within twenty feet of the car set an old tow truck with lights flashing and a dilapidated trailer parked on the shoulder in front of us. None of us had seen him arrive. The middle age driver wearing an old red T-shirt and jeans assured us of his help as long as we needed him but he was not equipped to haul us in. Then the car started again and he asked us to follow him to the next exit where there was a convenience store. He told us there was a Chrysler dealership and motels at exit 146 some miles up the hi-way. With the engine barely running we followed him to the store. There I noticed he was wearing a pistol in plain view. While we were deciding what to do he bought some snacks, cigarettes and $80.00 worth of instant lottery tickets. Definitely not my idea of an angel. The car was now running about normal and we decided to try for exit 146. Our friend still had some tickets to scratch but assured us he would be along shortly and would stop if we didn't make it. I watched for him in the mirror but didn't see him again. Just as we were exiting there he was pointing us in the direction of the motel. It had just gotten dark. We were safe. Those are the facts – What do you think??? Jim Mullett

P. S. The next day the car quit again in Tennessee so we were hauled to a dealership where we left it and bought another. It was Good Friday.

Beatitudes

Saturday evening and I am tired, almost too tired to answer Isabel's call to supper. Doc said my blood is low whatever that means but eat more liver. Come on Doc, you know I can't stand that stuff! Suddenly I remember I've forgotten all about inspiration so here I sit at my console totally empty and nothing to say. But this week I've been thinking about the Beatitudes and the first one says, **Blessed are the poor in spirit.** It's OK, silence is golden. You don't have to have the last word of wisdom. Just relax, the **Kingdom of Heaven** will be yours anyhow. Thanks Isabel for drying the dishes tonight....Jim

Peace Be With You

Palm Sunday; Luke nineteen; Jesus rides a donkey into Jerusalem, weeps over it and then cleanses the temple. Look at the parallels then and now in America. The masses are hailing a person who can give them the greatest mighty kingdom on the planet. People believe peace can be found through their own invincible Military Regiment. The Religious Institution has become an avenue of money and wealth. These are the things that cause Jesus to be sad. Verse 42 He says **If you had known, even you, especially in this your day, the things that make for your peace! But now they are hidden from your eyes**. He then continues to foretell the judgment to come on Jerusalem. Jesus said "**My house is a house of prayer".** Then, as now there were a few who knew Jesus intimately enough to be at peace with him. Some of them were women. Most were just common folks like you and me.....Jim Mullett

Snake in the Garden

There's a snake in my garden! It's the same reptile that invaded Eden and tempted Eve to take forbidden fruit. But I do have an advantage that Eve didn't have. The Devil's head has been crushed and his power taken away. The only strength he has over me is what I am willing to give him. Some folk go looking for the Devil under every rock so we can order him to leave the garden. The best way is to ignore him and turn our attention to Jesus, then the snake has no choice but to slither away. God is the Superpower and He grants mankind the ability to freely choose. The scripture I remind you of today is found in 1 Corinthians 10:13, **No temptation has overtaken you except such as is common to man; but God is faithful, who will not allow you to be tempted beyond what you are able, but with the temptation will also make the way of escape, that you will be able to bear it.** I use that promise a lot....Jim Mullett

Broken and in Trouble

Gospel of Mark chapter ten is a tough one. In America the family is broken and in trouble. Mom is at the job. The children are unsupervised and Dad is gone. Divorce and single parenting is rampant. This is not how God intended it to be. **Jesus said: from the beginning of the Creation God made them male & female. For this reason a man shall leave his father and mother and be joined to his wife. What God has joined together let not man separate.** Yet the devastation of divorce is upon us and Christian homes are not immune. Now what? We can't fix it ourselves but God's matchless Grace can see us through. To those caught in this web, pray this prayer: **Dear Lord take up the tangled strands where we have wrought in vain, that by the skill of thy dear hands some beauty may remain.** To the rest of us: If God in His love, mercy and forgiveness grants His child a second chance, we are not the judge. Having said that, I don't believe God can ever bless the guilty party in a love triangle unless true repentance takes place. Happiness is only found in His original intent.... Jim

Visitor at the Door

Last Sunday a visitor stood by the door of our church asking what is meant by The New Birth spoken of in John 3 to Nicodemus. Later I came home and read from Marks' Gospel chapter 7. Jesus said; **Out of the heart of man proceed evil thoughts, adulteries, fornications, murders, thefts, covetousness, wickedness, deceit, an evil eye, blasphemy, pride, foolishness**. All these evil things originate in the spiritual heart of man and will keep us out of Heaven. That's why we must be Born Again. God replaces that nature and gives us His own. It is the beginning of the pathway to Holiness without which no man will see the Lord. The New Birth cleans up an evil heart and forgives all our sins. Our life on earth is limited. To waste even a single day living in wickedness is pure folly. True Christianity is not dull....Jim Mullett

Lesson on Forgiveness

So while we were in Florida our home was ransacked, our truck taken out of the garage and left wrecked fifteen miles away and I missed the inspiration last Sunday. We needed to go home and secure what was left. So are there any lessons we can learn from living in a high crime rural area? Yes. First, forgiving the unknown culprit frees one from the anger one would normally experience from being so violated. However forgiveness should not free the criminal from the long arm of the law. The investigating officer told us "The law is not here to be forgiving". Second, relationships to God and Family are far more important than wealth. Our well-being and personhood must not be dependent on our possessions. **Paul said "I have learned in whatsoever state I am therewith to be**

content". Jesus said "do not lay up treasures on earth where thieves break in and steal, but lay-up treasure in Heaven. Where your treasure is there will your heart be also". Having said all that, I hope they catch this guy! Have a good day .... Jim

Given the Power

For a scripture basis this morning read Mark 3:13-19 and I would ask Jesus, why did you choose two guys like Peter and Judas? You sent them out to preach. You gave them both power to cast out demons and heal sickness yet when the chips were down both turned their back on you. Peter denied knowing you and Judas sold you to be killed. Verse thirteen simply says, **You wanted them**. If you wanted them it would be a clear indication you want us too and when we sin you are there to forgive us just like you did for Peter without even a word of chastisement. That's real love....better even than Valentine's Day....Jim

Free to Celebrate

Why, Why, Why? Reading Mark chapter two that word seems to be dominating. Why Jesus, do you break our Sabbath rules? Why do you eat with sinners? Why don't you and your disciples fast as we do and why did you speak blasphemy and tell that sick man his sins were forgiven? In response Jesus simply turned to the paralyzed sick man, healed him and sent him home, declaring, **that you may know that the Son of Man has power on earth**! The crowds glorified God. Levi quit his job collecting taxes. Jesus and His disciples went to dinner but those religious Scribes and Pharisees, consumed by hatred and envy plotted to kill their Lord. If our religion does not set us free to celebrate then we would do well to take a second look. Jim

The Good Shepherd

This morning the International Sunday School lesson is taken from the beautiful story of the good Shepherd in John chapter 10. Speaking of the sheep pen Jesus said **I am the door. If anyone enters by me, he will be saved, and will go in and out and find pasture.** He said **I am the good shepherd. The good shepherd gives His life for the sheep**. He said, **I know my sheep and am known by My own. He said other sheep I have which are not of this fold: them also I must bring and they will hear my voice and there will be one flock and one shepherd**. What a comforting, reassuring and intimate image of our life in Christ. Could it be that in our secular materialistic society you or I might be one of those "other" sheep? How lush and green is the grass in your pasture field? This world offers many substitutes but nothing can compare to the intimate and secure environment provided by our Good Shepherd. Have a happy day…Jim Mullett

4 Stages of Wisdom

For Christian parents who are concerned about the spiritual life of their adult children I give you the wisdom of Dr. Scott Peck. He writes in his book Denial of the Soul page 124 about stages of spiritual development. (I quote)

Stage 1, which I label Chaotic, Antisocial. In this more primitive stage people may appear either religious or secular, but either way, their belief system is profoundly superficial. It may be thought of as a stage of lawlessness.

Stage 2, which I label Formal, Institutional. This is the stage of the letter of the law in which religious fundamentalists (meaning most religious people) are to be found.

Stage 3, I label Skeptic, Individual. Here is where the majority of secularists are situated. People in this stage are usually scientific-minded, rational, moral and humane. Their outlook is predominantly materialistic. They tend to be not only skeptical of the spiritual but uninterested in anything that cannot be proven.

Stage 4, I have called mystical, Communal. In this most mature stage of religious development, which may be thought of as one of the spirit of the law, women and men are rational but do not make a fetish of rationalism. They have begun to doubt their own doubts. They feel deeply connected to an unseen order of things, although they cannot fully define it. They are comfortable with the mystery of the sacred. (End of quote)

So dear parent take comfort in Proverbs 22:6 **Train up a child in the way he should go, and when he is old he will not depart from it....** Jim

Testament Laws

In our Last Sunday School Class someone raised a good question; what was the purpose of all those Old Testament laws for the Hebrew people such as forbidding work on the Sabbath? I would counter with a question; When Jesus was born would there have been a Jewish Nation had it not been for the laws and rules? It is our perimeters that we accept for ourselves that gives us an identity. I cannot honestly call myself a Christian unless I accept and practice the life Jesus calls me to. It involves loving God, and my neighbor as myself. He calls on me to take up a cross and follow him. His rules are not as well defined as those in the Old Testament but then at our invitation He places His Holy Spirit into our heart with this promise; **The Holy Spirit whom the Father will send in my name, He will teach you all things. John 14:26** His presence becomes visible in our lives. The world can spot a phony very quickly. Sinners also recognize the rules....Blessings...Jim

Eternal Life

What is a Christian? CNN ask the question of a panel of the several popular pastors of large mega churches. A Christian was described as one who supports the nation of Israel, one who is in a battle against evil, one who is expecting the apocalypse, one who expects God to make him wealthy and another simply said one who loves all people. Only once at the end of the entire hour was there any mention of Jesus Christ. What a tragedy to identify ourselves with His name but not to recognize Him as the source of Eternal Life. He said "**I am the way, the Truth and the Life. No one comes to the Father except through me.** And in Matthew 7:22 Jesus said "**Many will say to me in that day, Lord, Lord have we not prophesied in Your name, cast out demons in Your name, and done many wonders in Your name? And I will declare to them, I never knew you, depart from me.** Be sure you are not following a wolf in sheep's clothing. Keep your eyes on Jesus. Learn to know Him....Jim

About Education

In his book "Denial of the Soul" Scot Peck says that "perhaps the most critical choice in people's lives is when and whether to discontinue their education". High School, Maybe College and then we're done. For Christians make sure we are saved and that's all that's necessary. How sad! A lazy mind will never **Press toward the goal for the prize of the upward call of God in Christ Jesus**. Philippians 3:14. God designed our lives so that we can know Him; the ultimate source of our life and the Creator of the Universe. How could He have designed a better environment for human learning then this life on Earth? What an exciting journey this quest for continuing education, but it's only for those who know they don't have all the answers. Happy Learning...Jim

Interstate 35

Interstate 35 runs from Southern Texas to Northern Minnesota. Now as CNN reports there is a pastor in Texas who has suggested this is the highway prophesied in Isaiah 35:8. **A highway shall be there and a road and it shall be called the Highway of Holiness**. Some Christians have faith that is indeed the case and have established prayer meetings along the roadway in six states. Here is an extreme example of people who allow others to do their thinking for them. They will believe anything, even a lie. Read the whole chapter. Isaiah is speaking of future glory created by God. **The desert shall rejoice and blossom like as the rose. The eyes of the blind shall be opened. The lame shall leap like a deer. Waters shall burst forth in the wilderness and streams in the desert**. It is a Holy Place, a place of beauty and bright colors. There are today groups of people who are told it is a sin to wear anything but plain clothing. They should read this chapter. Oh by the way: there is also a Route 35 that runs through our town here in Ohio. Why should Texas have a monopoly on Holiness? Thinking and praying go hand in hand...Jim

A Crown Restored

Wow! What a Christmas gift! There stood Miss USA, the queen of the greatest beauty pageant on earth, her crown crumbled and dirty at her feet, standing at the bar of judgment, Royalty gone amuck. Just like us, created in the image of God, joint heirs with Jesus Christ and destined to reign with him in the glorious and holy Kingdom of God but just like Tara we get caught up in the things this world has to offer. Sin separates us from our destiny and our crown is utterly defiled and dirty, we can wear it no more. But Wait! The babe in the manger is now the King, the owner of the pageant. He stoops and picks up the crown. He cleanses it and restores it back to its original luster and freely gives it back to us. Tara got another chance and so do we. How can we ever get a greater gift? That's love.....Jim

A Second Chance

Freely you have received, freely give. This is the instruction of Jesus in Matthew 10:8. Last week we wrote about God giving us a second chance to regain the position of Royalty that was lost in sin. Perhaps a New Year resolution now could be to offer a second chance to someone who has wronged us. There are broken relationships that could be restored if one was willing to forgive the wrongs and hurts we have experienced. A wise mentor once told me, "Always keep your relationships so the next move is up to the other person." The risk is always that we may get hurt all over again but the reward of a happier New Year might just be worth the challenge. Just something to think about...Happy New Year...Jim

Season of Advent

Verse 27 of the first chapter in the bible simply states, **God created man in His own image.** We are now in the season when our attention turns to a baby in a manger, a baby none other than God Incarnate. Therefore we must see ourselves in the life of that child. But wait there's a problem; a vast chasm between the baby and me called sin is blocking my vision. Before I can see myself in Christ there must be redemption by the Grace of God to solve the sin problem. After that happens my life will reflect who He is; love, joy, peace, patience, kindness, goodness, faithfulness, gentleness and self-control. **These are written that you may believe that Jesus is the Christ, the Son of God, and that believing you may have life in His name. John 20:31** Paul puts it another way; **Christ in you, the hope of glory**. Have a wonderful Christmas...Jim

The Love Chapter (modern version)

Today's Inspiration is not original with me. It came to me from one of you. I love it. It's a Christmas version of 1 Corinthians 13.

If I decorate my house perfectly with plaid bows, strands of twinkling lights and shiny balls, but do not show love to my family, I am just another decorator.

If I slave away in the kitchen baking dozens of Christmas cookies, preparing gourmet meals and arranging a beautiful adorned table at mealtime, but do not show love to my family, I am just another cook.

If I work at the soup kitchen, carol in the nursing home and give all that I have to charity, but do not show love to my family, it profits me nothing.

If I trim the spruce with shimmering angels and crocheted snowflakes, attend a myriad of holiday parties and sing in the choir's cantata but do not focus on Christ I have missed the point.

Love stops the cooking to hug the child. Love sets aside the decorating to kiss the husband. Love is kind though harried and tired. Love does not envy another's home that has coordinated Christmas china and table linens.

Love does not yell at the kids to get out of the way, but is thankful they are there to be in the way. Love does not only give to those who are able to give in return but rejoices in giving to those who can't.

Love bears all things, believes all things, hopes all things, endures all things. Love never fails. Video games break, pearl necklaces will be lost, golf clubs will rust, but giving the gift of love will endure. Merry Christmas and lots of love to you and yours. **...**Anonymous

<u>One of Us</u>

It's December and the season of Advent. While science debates how monkey became man Christians will debate how God became man. This Question starts in the Garden of Eden where Adam stood naked before God to answer that fearful question, Where art Thou? In Psalms 14 we all stand where Adam stood before Almighty God: **The Lord looks down from Heaven upon the children of men to see if there is any who understand, who seek God. They have all turned aside. They have together become corrupt. There is none who does good, no not one.** God knew the only way to save what He created was to become one of them. It was His decision to be born of Mary in a lowly stable. He came to serve the ones He loved. We have been redeemed...Jim

Our Statue of Liberty

A cartoon reads: Oranges $20.00 per dozen "picked by US Citizens". Oh the dilemma we are in. We want cheap produce but the people harvesting the crop must stay in their own country. I am happy that my Great Grandfather Mullett, though he had nothing, was welcomed into this country in 1833. Our invitation engraved on the Statue Of Liberty still proclaims, **"Bring me your tired, your poor, your huddled masses yearning to breathe free, the wretched refuse of your teaming shore. Send these, the home-less, tempest-tossed to me**." The immigrants that came accepted the most menial jobs and turned them into wealth. Now we fear the loss of our riches and therefore plan to build a seven hundred mile fence to keep the poor outside. Times have changed. My fellow Christians, I believe the one from whom we take our name is sad. Did He not instruct the Rich Young Ruler to "**Sell whatever you have and give to the poor and you will have treasure in Heaven: and come, take up the cross and follow me". Mark 10: 21**. It's certainly not a popular idea today but think about it…Jim

Our Dilemma as a Christian Nation

Last Sunday I wrote about our dilemma. As a Christian Nation what is our responsibility to the aliens in our Country? My friend Penny responded:

"Yes Jim. You know I like to stir up a bees nest! I think and I'd like to know others thoughts and solutions. It's all well and good to have ideals. I want to protect our Democracy as we've known it. Our Lord was center part of its creation. Mexico is a very wealthy country. She doesn't spread her wealth downward. She encourages her citizens to break our laws and rob our citizens. What are we being robbed of? Most illegals seek work at a lower pay. They collect social security, welfare, food stamps, low income housing, and their young people get into our universities for free. I believe if a system was set up, after the mass deportation, to provide a work permit for those men and women who want to work would be good. Employers should be forced to pay at least minimum wages. Yes we would have higher prices but all would benefit in the end".

So Please, I invite everyone to enter this discussion. Send me your comments this week and unless you tell me not to, I will include your concerns and / or solutions next week…Jim

Illegal Immigrants

I do want to thank those of you who responded to the message concerning illegal immigrants two weeks ago. Here again is a portion of the original text and following are your responses: **Our invitation engraved on the Statue Of Liberty still proclaims, "Bring me your tired, your poor, your huddled masses yearning to breathe free, the wretched refuse of your teaming shore. Send**

these, the homeless, tempest-tossed to me." Do we still practice what we preach?

Karen from Canada Writes:

Well Jim! Although I am in another country, I know we serve the same Lord. It seems to me that Jesus welcomed all who would come, no matter their station in life. Didn't He say "As you do unto the least of these, so do you unto me"? I think that He would see us give aid, a helping hand, rather than "mass deportation". Let us not forget that we were all immigrants once!

Doug from Columbus, Ohio writes:

Given a choice, most people will take the path of least resistance. Unfortunately, the legal route is not currently easier to follow than the illegal route. We attempted to work through our immigration and naturalization services (INS) to get 6 month work visas for Manuel and Beto. They had housing, jobs, and transportation lined up. We filled out stacks of paperwork, and sent several hundred dollars to the INS. Other than the cashed check, we never obtained as much as a letter of confirmation that they had even received our paperwork. The INS office that we had to deal with was in St. Louis. Living 500 miles from there made it just that much more difficult. We sent multiple letters of inquiry, and phone calls never seemed to make it to the person who could help us out. The alternative method is quite simple. In most any city in the U.S. there are people ready and willing to supply fake identities and everything needed to setup residence illegally. Most of these cases are family or friends who already live here offering the services for free. You don't have to deal with a stranger 500 miles away who doesn't even have the common courtesy to return a phone call after they've collected hundreds of your dollars. Until our government fixes the bureaucracy involved in working here legally, they will continue to miss out on tax dollars that could be collected from legally working immigrants. As long as immigrants are working illegally with fake identities at below minimum wage jobs our civic services will continue to be strained. Even if they don't pay out to the illegal immigrant, the children that they bear here are US citizens and entitled to social services. Bottom line; make it easier for anybody who wants to work here to do it legally so we can collect taxes. Pay them a decent wage so that they are less of a strain on social services.

Wanda from Jackson writes:

Now think about this…if we do a mass deportation, who will pick all of our oranges and work for very low pay doing the jobs none of us are willing to do? It would devastate our economy, not to mention all of those yummy oranges would go to waste. We need the immigrants. Why not make them legal citizens provided they are willing to work and contribute to our tax system? I would rather use my tax dollars to pay for an illegal immigrant child to have routine medical care including immunizations than to build bombs and keep sending our money and troops to Iraq. Is it so terrible for the Mexican parent to want a better life for their children? The Mexican immigrant risks their life in hope for a better standard of living, many times leaving family behind. They come here to work and send the majority of the money back to the family in Mexico. Would it not be better for the family to also live here thus keeping the money here in our country? Also if they are legal citizens, they pay into our social security system, payroll taxes etc. and help boost our economy. I say give the Mexicans a break. All of us would do the same thing they are doing if we were in their unfortunate situation.

Jonathan from Pennsylvania writes:

Hey Jim,

You won't know me, although you met some of my siblings at the Cross Roads reunion. Having worked in a third world country for over 30 years, I continue to find the misinformation that most Usans have tragic. (Persons from other countries in the "Americas" find the use of the term "American" insensitive to the fact that they too are "Americans", and so I have coined the word Usan to refer to persons who are citizens of the USA). I would ask each of us to become friends of the poor and oppressed in so much of Latin America, and to live with them in the "little towns" or their "favelas" or "shacks" or whatever, and experience their generosity before we give easy solutions to a very complex problem. Paraguay (where I lived and worked among the poorest) suffered incredibly from the control and might of a US sponsored dictator for over 30 years. For the past 4 years the duly elected president, a firm Christian, and his wife one of the charter members of a Mennonite Church, has governed the country. But corruption, greed, selfishness and poverty are worse than ever, and hundreds of thousands of Paraguayans have left the country in search of survival. (Moral: the problem is very complex, and one man, or woman, cannot solve it ever, because change must happen in the heart of all persons). Mexico is by far not the only country whose citizens look for survival in the US. I cannot conceive of a committed Christian consciously wanting to condemn persons, who most often are looking to survive, not to having a 2nd or 3rd car, or any car, to return to hungry crying children. When you have sat at your table, and had children watching, through your window, watching each bite enter your mouth, and their mother telling you they have not eaten for 2 days, then you will be qualified to send them away empty, "for as much as you did it not unto the smallest of these, you did it not to me," said Jesus. Please, let us open our heart, and let God's incredible compassion soften it more than our "loyalty" to a non-reality, even in the US.

Special Thanks

My special thanks to each one of you who took the time to respond to this message this past month. It is people like you who make a difference. Solomon in Ecclesiastes 12:13 says: **Let us hear**

the conclusion of the whole matter; Fear God and keep his commandments for God will bring every work into judgment. We who have experienced God's love and forgiveness now become responsible to demonstrate that same love which, as Jesus taught, knows no national boundaries. We need to influence our Nation to find a better solution to our problem of illegal immigration then simply building walls and fences. By reaching out to the less fortunate, America can enhance its image rather than destroy it. As indicated in your responses our present bureaucracy is simply not working for them or us. Perhaps a better way would be to turn the process over to the business community. Allow employers to issue government sponsored work permits to fill their employment needs. Require payment of at least the minimum wage and offer free education so when the time limits run out a person is equipped to return to the homeland and make a difference. Limit our government to screening out the criminal element. I just wonder how Jesus would solve it....Jim

Grand Frustration

This past week I experienced a grand frustration. I was standing at an overlook, camera in hand and trying to capture an adequate image of the blazing Fall colors in the Blue Ridge Mountains of North Carolina. The pictures are nice but can never be a substitute for standing on top of Grandfather Mountain and there experiencing the grandeur of God's Creation. Nor can one fully explain to another the rapture of a personal Spiritual moment in the presence of Almighty God but I can say that it doesn't just happen. For Isabel and I to get to that overlook on the parkway took discipline and a strong resolve stemming from desire. There was the drudgery of packing and unpacking a suitcase. There were long tiring hours of driving the Interstates. Lodging and food is not cheap in those hills so the value of our dollars became secondary. In our quest for that glorious moment Jesus is our example: **Who for the joy that was set before Him endured the cross and has sat down at the right hand of the Throne of God. Let us lay aside every weight and run with endurance the race that is set before us. Hebrews 12: 1-2… Jim**

Two Men Died

Two men died, both of which I was intimately acquainted. Both were men of faith and met their death with calm and confidence. I believe today both are with the Lord so what's the big deal? The difference is in how they used and lived their time on earth. God likes variety and these two men were vastly different. One seen himself as a man with limited social graces and appeal and although there were dreams of self-development no serious attempt at improvement was ever made. Instead to protect himself from a hostile world he drew a circle around himself and lived his life within his own fences.

The other man left his circle wide open. It left him vulnerable; people could and did take advantage of him but with an open circle the whole world was at his door. He became a wealthy man, not counted in dollars and land but in human relationships and the enjoyment of all that God created. He was a man with vision that looked beyond the challenges of life for the victory and the joy of living.

My favorite scripture today is Philippians 3:14. **I press toward the mark for the prize of the high calling of God in Christ Jesus**. (KJV) Don't look for pie in the sky bye and bye or wait on happiness until you win the lottery or go to heaven. The prize is just outside your circle; travel, volunteer for community service, start a bible class, visit the elderly, give an unexpected gift, use your imagination, open the door and **go for it**.

Blessings to you this week. You get this one day early because I'm going out of town to attend a funeral.... Jim Mullett

Spiritual Growth

Spiritual growth happens in the present, not the future or the past. This past winter a friend gave me a book purported to be so amazing you can't put it down. It was about a "holy" man in China living a very miraculous life. Last week another book came to my box free and unsolicited: God has returned incarnate in a man, the Bible is now irrelevant for we have entered the Age of the Kingdom! All this in China, but where in China and who wrote this stuff? The book sounds dramatic but is impossible to authenticate. We live at a time when many Christians get all excited about end time reports. The "Left Behind" series made millionaires of its authors. When the disciples ask about end times **Jesus said "take heed that no one deceives you for many will come in my name saying I am the Christ"** This week read Matthew 24:1-14. Our job is found in verse 14. Oh yes, I had another offer this week: for twenty five bucks I can buy a CD that will identify the antichrist and 666. A Hungry person called last evening needing food. I think that will be a better investment... Jim

God Asks Us This Question

In Isaiah 50 God asks us this question: **Is My hand shortened at all that it cannot redeem? Or have I no power to deliver?** Today I find myself concerned and fearful about the direction a close friend is taking in life. I've spent a number of days worrying and scheming to think up a plan of intervention. Isn't that so human of all of us? I know God is much superior in wisdom and knowledge then I am but suppose he tells me to stay out of it and just continue to be loving? This really tests our confidence in God. Can I trust and not be afraid? ..... Jim

In A Different World

My son is a computer networking engineer. When he graduated from High School I would have ask, a WHAT? As a lad he brought a friend along to church. Today Cory is a pastor in intercity Columbus, Ohio and a partner in the ministry of Christ's Gospel. He has a lovely website. Again I would have ask, what's that? We seniors are in a different world today than in the past. The Internet and all this new technology provide an excellent avenue of communicating the Good News. The internet and Acts 1:7&8 go hand in hand. **It is not for you to know the times or seasons which the Father has put in His own authority. But you shall receive power when the Holy Spirit has come upon you: and you shall be witnesses to me to the end of the earth.** Do you think perhaps God may have provided the knowledge and expertise that resulted in the design of this new world? Jim

Must Be Born Again

I just again read John chapter three about Jesus, his discussion with Nicodemus and the declaration "**Ye Must Be Born Again**". Nicodemus was confused. He was a Pharisee, a Ruler of the Jews and the rule book was the Law of Moses, especially the Ten Commandments. He was taught that keeping the rules was how you would be saved. That's how it was in the Old Testament under

Moses but now Jesus speaks of being Born of the Spirit. God loves you He declares in verse sixteen. I paid the price for your sins. If you believe in me you will not perish but have eternal life. We can trust in Jesus for our salvation or we can trust ourselves to keep the rules. It's your choice. You can't have it both ways.... Jim

My Greater Concern

I got a letter this week from our Missionaries in Argentina. It seems persons they're ministering to are concerned about the U.S. trusting in arms of destruction and that by their silence our churches are also responsible. My greater concern is that far too many Christians are openly encouraging and supporting our present warfare! It's a natural animal instinct to stake out and defend one's own territory. We humans are smarter than animals; we have created weapons to kill more efficiently. The Pelage People in South America are being taught to apply Jesus' values and teachings to the clamor for justice. The struggle for Life in its fullness must be part of our discipleship. Jesus said **"I have come that they may have life and that they may have it more abundantly"** John 10: 10. Our secular world knows nothing but warfare but we who are followers of Christ must never be silent with the message of God's love to all people. Think about it...Jim Mullett

The Heartbroken Prophet

Jeremiah was a heartbroken prophet with a heartbreaking message. Forty years, despised and persecuted by his countrymen he bathes his harsh prophecies in tears of compassion. Jesus also wept over Jerusalem and I believe He weeps today over the brutality of the Middle East and the way Christian people have misinterpreted His Kingdom. He stood before Pilot and rightly declared Himself to be the King of the Jews. The Scriptures clearly designate Him to sit on the throne of David. But He said to Pilot **"My Kingdom is not of this world".** In Luke 17: 21 Jesus said **"Indeed the Kingdom is within you".** Jesus as a direct descendant from Abraham fulfilled God's promise that all nations would be blessed through Him, not only the descendants of Abraham but everyone including the Arabs. In Luke 12 Jesus said "**Do not fear little flock, for it is your Fathers good pleasure to give you the Kingdom.** This war today is a human battle. I doubt that God has anything in it. It leaves me feeling sad…Jim Mullett

Cast Down O My Soul

Wow its Friday PM and we just returned from five wonderful days in Ontario visiting friends and relatives. Now reality hits: The raccoons destroyed the sweet corn patch, the grass is too long, the mower is still in the repair shop not fixed, you wouldn't believe all the bills in the accumulated mail, a good friend died while we were gone and it's starting to rain! Time to get out the good book and read Psalm 42. **Why are you cast down O my soul? Hope in God for I shall yet praise Him for the help of his countenance.** OK I read it and I do have Faith. I shall not be overwhelmed forever. Tomorrow is a new day and God is still alive! So we all have our days, don't we? Thank God it is not a lasting thing......Jim

To See Jesus

In August I began a study to see Jesus from seven various perspectives as written by Brian McLaren in his book, A Generous Orthodoxy. Through this study I discovered a Jesus who is too large to fit into the box that I so often create for Him. I am reminded of the words of Paul in 1 Corinthians 3:11, **No other foundation can anyone lay then that which is laid which is Jesus Christ.** Yet we build our lives on our own ambitions, desires and understanding. We applaud war and destruction and only pay lip service to the Prince of Peace. I believe it is time for the Christian to get back to the basics of what our Lord taught us: Non-violent love, Liberator of the oppressed, Giver of life, Healing and forgiveness for us sinners, Servants of humanity. Come with me as we explore several of these different aspects of who Jesus is. Blessings to you...Jim

The Roman Catholic Jesus

As a young adolescent I was sure anyone not of my faith was going to Hell, especially Catholics. When my older brother announced that he was dating one I assumed he would also end up in the fire. Brian McLaren speaks of seven Jesus' he learned to know. I would call Him the Jesus of Seven Faiths. One is the **Roman Catholic Jesus**. Catholics are aware of a human race that is bound up in hatred, envy, greed, lust, murder and war. All this can lead only to a fearful death and separation from God but the Jesus they worship overcame death in the Resurrection and set us free from the grip of evil. He even set me free from the bigotry of my youth! I believe true Catholics would greet us as Paul did in Titus 1:4 **Grace, mercy and peace from God the Father and the Lord Jesus Christ our Savior!** Next week we'll take a look at the Conservative Protestant Jesus. Blessings for the week…Jim Mullett

The Conservative Protestant Jesus

The wages of sin is death! How I would tremble with fear of those words until after each offence I would turn to the **Conservative Protestant Jesus**. He died on the cross to somehow absorb the punishment I deserved for breaking the rules. I suspect He even forgave some conservative preachers and bishops who created rules not found in the Holy Scriptures! This Jesus will be my attorney when

I stand before the Judgment of God. **"We must all appear before the judgment seat of Christ"** 2 Corinthians 5:10. This Jesus carries my guilt and for that I praise Him but does this emphasis on His death marginalize His life; His wise teachings and kind deeds, the Beatitudes and the Sermon on the Mount, His compassion for the poor and hurting people He met? Brian McLaren said, "In my heart grew a deep, subtle, unspoken sense that something was missing which gradually opened my heart to search for other ways of seeing Jesus" Next week let's look at the Eastern Orthodox Jesus.... Jim Mullett

<u>The Greek Orthodox Jesus</u>

There is an eternal celebration going on between Father, Son and Holy Spirit but because of sin the world is missing out. God entered our broken world through the **Eastern Orthodox Jesus** to teach us the joys of Creation. Jesus became human to show us how to be included in this "dance" with the Trinity. Our great sin is that we are so exclusive in our denominational religion and American culture. Those not like us we call outsiders and foreigners. Even Christians debate whether we should "kick out" the illegal aliens. Jesus, in His humanity saves the world by showing us the way back to Eden or is it the way forward to the Paradise of God spoken of in Revelation 2:7 **To him who overcomes I will give to eat from the Tree Of Life which is in the midst of the Paradise of God.** Like us this Orthodox Jesus lived in the span between. May we learn something from Him? Next week we we'll look at the Liberal Protestant Jesus....Jim

The Liberal Protestant Jesus

My dear friend Anne has gone to be with the Lord but while she lived she had no problem whatever with the Old Testament story of Abraham sacrificing Isaac: God would never instruct him to do that! Abraham just misunderstood the instruction! Miracles like Jesus feeding 5000 with a lad's lunch may or may not have happened. More important is the lesson we learn from the story. Jesus will supply our needs! She was very sincere in her worship of the **Liberal Protestant Jesus.** His example and teaching inspired her to work compassionately for social justice, even more so than most fundamentalists. She lived alone but took her ex-husband into her home and nursed him through his terminal illness. Anne was wealthy having received a $100,000.00 inheritance but she gave it all away a few dollars at a time anytime she met someone in need. Just before she died she expressed concern to me that she had kept one thousand dollars for final expenses. Someone may need it more than she. Her body was donated to science. She heard the words of Jesus **"In as much as you have done it unto one of the least of these My brethren you did it to Me"** Matthew 25:40...Her friends planted a tree in her memory.... Jim

The Pentecostal / Charismatic Jesus

Oh how we must learn to discern the difference of feelings that come from the human emotional soul and the voice of God speaking to and through our spirit. The best way is to test the spirit with a stable body of believers. The **Pentecostal / Charismatic Jesus** teaches us how to receive miracles and healings from God through faith in His promises. Brian McLaren states "the Pentecostal Jesus also saves by his powerful presence in this present moment". The Holy Spirit today is no less than the real presence of Jesus invading a world bound by sin, sickness and poverty. We need to meet this Jesus but be careful; the Devil does not want you to know Him so he clouds the issue with the theological debate over the gift of tongues. Be ready for it but avoid the debate. It's not a sign of spiritual maturity. Trust the truth of the scriptures: **Every good gift and every perfect gift is from above and comes down from the Father of lights.** James 1:17.....Next week meet the Anabaptist Jesus...Jim

The Anabaptist Jesus

More wars have been fought in the name of religion then we can count. God is on our side rings the battle cry and then we go to kill and slaughter the enemy. How we need **The Anabaptist Jesus** to teach us how to live in peace. Remember in Luke 9: 51–56 how James and John wanted to call fire from Heaven to destroy the

Samaritans. Jesus rebuked them! **You don't know what manner of spirit you're of**. The human race is divided and violent and needs to learn the ways of Christ. Jesus supersedes the Old Testament by teaching the Grace of God and the way of love in human relations. Read the Sermon on the Mount in Matthew chapter 5 - 7. Today he has convened a learning community of disciples who seek to model lives of love and peace. They are called Conscientious Objectors to military service. Nowhere does Jesus teach us to go to war. Next week we look at the Jesus of liberation theology… Jim

The Jesus of Liberation Theology

We hear much in the news of the (CPT) Christian Peacekeeper Teams. Recently Tom Fox was murdered in Iraq while serving the **Jesus of Nonviolent Liberation Theology.** Humanity is oppressed by corrupt powers and regimes. This Jesus uses bands of activists to confront the evil systems of this world and bring in the Peace of God. In our own time and Nation it was many brave people standing firm but without violence and absorbing the hatred of Southern Segregation against a people who had long been denied their Constitutional Civil Rights. Somehow even professing Christians were among the most violent and hateful. The churches were and still are among the hardest institutions to integrate. **It was this Jesus who went to the synagogue proclaiming Himself to preach the gospel to the poor, heal the brokenhearted and set at liberty**

those who are oppressed. His own people threw him out but still he invites us to bear the cross with him. Oh but doing it His way could get you killed! For safety sake we would rather go to war and toss bombs at each other. You can read it in Luke chapter four….Jim

Evolution and the Bible

I heard it again this week: "If you don't believe God created the universe in six days you believe in evolution" True statement? That depends: Do you mean evolution of the universe or the evolution of life? Go back with me to Genesis chapter one. Verse one says "**God created the heaven and the earth**" Bingo, no debate! God created the universe. Now God speaks and things change. In verse twenty one the universe has now changed to the point where it can support life on planet Earth. God now in verse 21 performs His second creative act when **He creates life** and places it in the oceans just where science claims it began and in verse 24 God instructs the **Earth to bring forth the living creature**. His third and last creative act is in verse 27: **God created man in His own image**. We need more Bible believing Christians to commit themselves to a serious and open minded study of science. There is a beautiful harmony between science and the Bible. The more important question however; how do you reflect the Image of God in which you were created? I invite your comments… Jim Mullett

Amazing Grace

Amazing Grace! Mostly we only think of it in relation to our salvation. I believe it also is a miraculous factor in our physical survival. As a young teenage "chemist" I learned that combining certain common household items produced a gas. Mix these items in a bottle and plug it; the cork would soon be blown high in the sky. My next experiment was to cap the bottle. I set it on a fence post, ran back about a hundred feet and waited; and waited. Finally I started edging closer for a better look until I was within eight or ten feet. Perhaps the cap was not tight enough and the pressure leaked off but how could I know? Should I pick it up and release the cap? After some time of debate I decided to walk away and leave it. Within fifteen seconds behind me there was a loud explosion. I whirled around and the fence was invisible in a white cloud of gas. The bible says **"It is appointed to man once to die"** Only once. All other times there is God's loving Grace protecting us. Grace cannot be explained by science or natural law. It is a miracle of God directed to us for our safety and spiritual growth. Have a good week….Jim

Defining Spiritual Maturity

I have heard people brag about their superior spirituality. A scripture comes to mind: **Let him who thinks he stands take heed lest he fall, 1 Corinthians 10:12**. How can we define Spiritual

Maturity? I would call it "A constant attempt to be in harmony with God" Spiritual growth is a slow lifelong process of a search for Truth in an arena beyond science. It must be a walk of Faith. It is something we experience as a paradox. On one side it is very humbling to live in the presence of Almighty God. On the other side it is a tremendously uplifting experience. Abraham spent his life looking for a city that was out of this world. This week take time to meditate on Hebrews chapters 11 & 12.

As for us, the Mullett family is creating memories at Myrtle Beach. This was our Christmas gift to our children and grandkids. See you again next Sunday…Jim

Phenomenon of Love

Do we find life as a problem to be solved or a mystery to be lived? Far too often life becomes an all-consuming problem! We are born with an aggressive "me first" nature. Our Capitalistic culture teaches that what I can earn is mine to enjoy. Our greed takes over and we lay up for our future security much more than what is needed even at the expense of others. Add a bit of fear and we can soon become a nation of warring individuals even willing to kill. The Prince of Peace tells us in Matthew 13:11 **"It has been given to you to know the mysteries of the Kingdom Of Heaven"**. One of those mysteries is the phenomenon of Love. Not only the romantic kind that traps us into marriage but the love that prompts us to live by the Golden Rule, doing to others as we would have them do to us; everyone even our enemies. Returning good for evil is a mystery that can change the human heart and even perhaps the heart of a Nation but it starts in a solitary individual life, perhaps your life. Think about it….. Jim

Vulnerability

How much risk are you willing to assume? But when we become vulnerable might we not become wounded? Indeed yes, vulnerability requires us to be open. There is no way we can live a rich life unless we are willing to suffer depression and despair, fear and anxiety, throw in anger and the agony of forgiving, criticism and even rejection. I doubt if any of us can match the Lord Jesus when it comes to voluntarily accepting risk. But then He tells us in 2 Corinthians 12:9 **My grace is sufficient for you, for My strength is made perfect in weakness.** When we make ourselves vulnerable the effect on others will almost invariably be disarming. Strength controls people but Wounded Healers can change the heart. Have a good week…Jim

Persistence

So when do we reach the highest point in our life? Where is your personal pinnacle? Have we set any goals to reach for? The Apostle Paul said "**I press for the prize of the high calling of God in Christ**

Jesus" (KJV) Philippians 3:14. But so often we fail miserably! If Edison had quit at failure 1000 he never would have invented the light bulb but every failure taught him something that brought him closer to his goal. We need that kind of persistence if we are going to mature in our Christian life. At age eleven I publicly made the following pledge: "**All I am, all that I possess, all of which I am capable, every act, every word, every thought, every emotion, all are His and shall be His forever, come what may I am the Lords.**" Many periods of my life I forgot all about that pledge but occasionally I keep coming back to it. When our ultimate goal is the high calling of God in Christ Jesus it takes an entire lifetime and at the end God Himself will lift us to the pinnacle. Don't miss that call….. Jim

Technology of the Future

Several days ago I found myself very much intrigued by a small piston driven engine. It was totally sealed with no fuel lines, no intake or exhaust yet there it was rapidly spinning a flywheel and powered by nothing but heat from the sun. In our polluted environment this is technology of the future. In Genesis 2:15 God placed man into a beautiful unspoiled garden called Eden and gave him instruction to **tend and keep it.** Today our garden is called Planet Earth and we still have the same instructions. As citizens today we can hardly avoid the use of fossil fuels but we can plant the flowers and dispose of our trash, maybe even develop a lifestyle that would not produce so much refuse. Remember also that God has given to us and our children a mind that can be educated to develop new and better energy sources. God has provided for all we need to keep this garden beautiful and healthy. Blessings for the week…Jim

In the Season

We are in the season of Lent and Mardi Gras. Of sin and Redemption. Do I have any words of wisdom on the subject? No, none whatsoever! The apostle Paul in 1 Corinthians chapter one says the Gospel is not preached by words of wisdom but by the message of the Cross of Christ. **The message of the Cross is foolishness to those who are perishing but to those of us who are being saved it is the power of God**: Verse 18. Our Salvation is an act of God starting at the Cross 2000 years ago when he loved us enough to die and pay the penalty for the sins of the entire human race. When I recognize myself as a sinner and accept that atonement I am completely forgiven for all my sin. I am made holy and fit for Heaven. As I then grow and mature in the Faith Mardi Gras and all its allure fades into oblivion. A simple prayer will do; Lord, be merciful to me, a sinner. May God Bless…. Jim

My Rock

The Lord lives! Blessed be my Rock! Let the God of my Salvation be exalted. Psalms 18:46. What more can I say this Easter Sunday? Mark these words of David in your bible and carry this knowledge with you in the coming days. Meditate on it and give thanks...God is alive...Jim

Followers

It was Blue Jean Sunday, March 26, 2006. There was not a suit or tie in sight. It was a day to wear clean work clothes in honor of all the volunteers who served with the Mennonite Disaster Service. Eighteen months ago Hurricane Charlie had ripped through Desoto County leaving a trail of unbelievable destruction. Pine Creek Chapel opened their church to serve as headquarters. A topnotch commercial kitchen on wheels rolled into position as did a shower and bath facility. A new dormitory was built to house the workers. RV hookups and sewers appeared behind the church for long term staff and then they came, a new wave every week offering free labor to the destitute. 160 home were either totally rebuilt or repaired. Arcadia, Florida has shared in the Vision Statement of Mennonite Church USA: **God calls us to be followers of Jesus Christ and, by the power of the Holy Spirit, to grow as communities of grace, joy and peace, so that God's healing and hope flow through us**

to the world. After 2000 years Jesus still makes a difference.... Blessings for the week...Jim Mullett

Passion Week

From the Living Bible, Luke 19: 28-44 the fickle crowd was hailing Jesus as their new King. They wanted more miracles, more free food and physical healings and surely, supernatural defeat to their Roman enemies. Now they would live on easy street. But as they came closer to Jerusalem and he saw the city ahead Jesus began to cry. "Eternal peace was within your reach and you turned it down," he wept. "Now it is too late, for you have rejected the opportunity God offered you". Thought for today: Inner peace, right now amid all our problems and troubles is possible. Jesus taught the way in the Gospels. You too can find the way if you are willing to put in the time and effort. A good secular article to read was found in April 2000 issue of Readers Digest Page 97, Secrets of a Life Well Lived. Five points:

1. Lend yourself to Love.
2. Quit your job if it's not ethical.
3. See America
4. Lighten your load
5. Encourage a child.

This life, your life, is too precious to only be second rate.

Happy Trails – Jim Mullett

Inexhaustible Appetite

What a relief, tax day has passed for another year. Have we been reminded of our poverty or was it our wealth? One thing is sure; our government has an inexhaustible appetite for our dollars. It seems the national debt is out of control. As of today the debt exceeds 8.3 Trillion dollars or $28,058.14 for every man, woman and child in our country. Take your calculator and try to figure out how far back in history 8.3 trillion seconds would take us. If you can find the answer please e-mail it to me, I gave up. I'm just curious. As Christians might we be called to live a simpler lifestyle and make it our goal to personally be out of debt? In Matthew 5:5 Jesus said **the meek will inherit the earth**. Might this become our lot and responsibility if or when the United States can no longer pay up? Don't let that day take you unaware, each day we spend 2.2 billion dollars more then we take in. Oh let me see, is this inspiration or a challenge??

Think about it...Jim Mullett

Toolbox for Discipline

Our Spirituality is the engine that drives us to joyfully succeed in our life journey. Consider wisdom to be the steering mechanism. Scott Peck in his first book "The Road Less Traveled" speaks of self-discipline as the means of spiritual growth. It does not come easy or by means of a great revival as some Christians would like to believe.

In fact Peck does not necessarily make it an issue of Christianity. He gives us four tools of discipline that lead to our spiritual evolution:

1 The ability and will to delay gratification.

2. Accepting responsibility for our own life and action.

3. Dedication to truth and reality.

4. Balancing which he defines as extraordinary flexibility required for successful living in all spheres of activity.

He describes the book as "A New Psychology of Love, Traditional Values and Spiritual Growth". Peck embraced Christianity and was baptized some years after he wrote the book. I recommend it to all who like me have not yet fully arrived… Jim

Father of the Year

And a very special Father's Day it is. Yesterday I turned on the radio and learned I was chosen Father of the Year in our community. I humbly accept the honor and all the nice gifts that come with it: A weekend retreat at a state lodge, A 119 piece tool set, Golf clubs and an outing for the entire family and the list goes on including a one hour massage. So what's the deal that makes a good dad? In a nutshell I would say, accept responsibility for your mistakes and don't repeat them. Establish and keep the family traditions. Example: Many years ago in the Christmas Season we choose a nice

restaurant beside a lake for a meal and gift exchange. I heard our daughter exclaim, this is great, and we ought to do this every year. We haven't missed a year since; same restaurant, same waitress who also is involved in the gift exchange. Above all practice your Faith, don't just talk about it, be real in your lifestyle. Your kids are smarter than you might think. They will reflect who you are. My first bible memory assignment in school was Ephesians 6: 1-4. Look it up .....
Jim Mullett

Paradox

Paradox: Is this a one way or a two way street? The Ten Commandments say, **remember the Sabbath day to keep it Holy**. Jesus said **The Sabbath was made for man, not man for the Sabbath**. Mark 2:27. Shall I serve the Church or shall the Church serve me? When you go to church one should expect to be inspired by the music and hymns, by Spirit filled preaching and teaching, in the communion sacraments, by the fellowship of friends and even perhaps by the architecture. The Spirit of God finding and entering us in church and continuing in us through the week keeps us Holy. That's a one-way street. When we maintain the church with our tithes and talents we also assume responsibility. You will never find a perfect church but in the church you can find a perfect God. Have a great week...Jim

Young Love

Be My Valentine! How those words would stir the emotions during those school day romances and still bring pleasant smiles today. It is the beautiful love stories of the Bible that catch my attention today. The story of Ruth and Naomi; her mother-in law, both widows and how Naomi directs the younger Ruth in finding lifelong love with the man Boaz. This Tuesday you can find the Old Testament book of Ruth well worth the time it takes to read it. And then there is the heartbreak of Hosea married to Gomer and raising a family in spite of her constant infidelity. When she leaves him and finds herself sold as a slave he remains faithful and committed and buys her back. In Ephesians five the Apostle Paul alludes to the greatest love story of all time when he instructs men to **love as Christ loved the Church and gave himself** for it. Love is about the Golden Rule: Do unto others as you would have them do to you. It is God's solution for many of our problems. Giving ourselves to another adds a nice dimension to our life that cannot be achieved any other way.... Blessings for the week.....Jim.

Three Questions

Three questions every thinking person struggles with: **Who Am I? How did I get here? And for what purpose?** Paul tells us in Ephesians 2:10 we are His (God's) workmanship. In First

Thessalonians 5:23 he prays for complete sanctification of our spirit, our soul and our body. Like God we are a trinity. God is a Spirit therefore it is in the realm of our spirit that we are created in His image. Like Him, we are Eternal and Immortal. Through our spirit we have the capacity to worship and be inspired. In Genesis He breathed into man the Breath of Life (His life) and man became a living soul. When Adam sinned he died spiritually. That's why Jesus told Nicodemus, you must be born again. When we accept Jesus as our Savior God again breathes His life into our spirit. The next time you introduce yourself think how wonderful you really are! In the image of God! Next week: how did I get here? ...Jim

Master Planner

So how did we get here? In Psalms 139 David said, **you formed my inward parts: You covered me in my mother's womb. I will praise you for I am fearfully and wonderfully made: marvelous are your works**. Was it just a biological accident? No. There was a Master Planner that designed and created me. God's method in the natural universe is to plant a small seed and let it grow. The small acorn in 100 years develops into a large and stately tree. Given enough time and loving care a 200 pound human being develops from a microscopic cell. Even the Kingdom of Heaven, Jesus said is like a small mustard seed that grows and develops but when it comes to evolution many Christian people will become defensive.

One thing is sure, God made us; we didn't just happen. Could it be that God made this universe with just the right stuff that under His watchful care and direction it developed over billions of His eternal kind of days and years? Let's not miss God's words in Genesis 1:24 where He said "**Let the earth bring forth** the living creature. Next week: Why did He do it? What is the purpose of my existence? Think about these things....Jim

An Object of Affection

So what was in the mind of God when He created mankind and placed us on this earth? What is His purpose for my existence? Is it to do something great for Him? I don't think so. One universal rule is "love, to be love, must have an object for its affection". Today read 1 John 4: 7-11 which states specifically that "***God Is Love***". In our physical life our basis for love and affection is rooted in our sexuality. Could it be that in God there is a divine, holy and spiritual aspect of sexuality and we have been created in that image of Him? When He said "**it is not good for man to be alone**" was He speaking from His own experience? It is also not good for God to be alone. His purpose for us then must be to freely love Him in return, not because we have to but because we choose to. The great evil of this world is that we have not learned how to love each other. Therefore we cannot love God. Is there any individual in this world that you would die for? God's love for you is very real. Enjoy the romance this week...Jim

Walking Life's Road

M Scott Peck said; "Life is complex. There are no self-help manuals, no formulas and no easy answers. The right road for one is the wrong road for the other. It is a rocky path through the wilderness". Jesus said: **My sheep hear my voice and they follow Me**. John 10:27. In Matthew 18 we have the beautiful story of one lonely sheep that lost its way and how the Good Shepherd goes into the mountains seeking and finding the helpless stray. We can walk life road with confidence knowing somebody bigger than you or me cares enough to watch over us. There will at times be difficult portions in our pathway that we would rather avoid. Meet your problems head on; it's easy to get lost in a detour. Happy Trails.... Jim

Investing Your Time

About 2600 years ago in present day Iraq a King built a huge statue unto himself and demanded that all his subjects worship it; Daniel chapter three. Thank God for a Constitution that grants us separation of Church and State! Shelley once wrote a poem describing the remains of a statue in the desert. Inscribed on the pedestal: "My name is Ozymandias, King of Kings: Look on my works, ye might, and despair!" Yet all that is left of the statue is two vast trunk- less legs of stone and an obscure face half buried in the sand. Our life on earth is limited but the memories we create today will live on in the hearts of the next generation. Investing your time and influence into a child is of far greater value than leaving behind a large estate. Can you think of anything in history that has outlasted the stories of the Bible? Blessings today…Jim

New Year

Wow! A brand new gift from our Creator God or is it just an illusion related to Father Time? To answer I will take you to Revelation 21:5 where **He who sat on the Throne said, "Behold I make all things new**". In verse one John even saw a new Heaven and a new earth. Today we receive a New Year perfect before us and without blemish. As we walk through it we will leave as a part of history all of our actions good as well as bad. In the book of Daniel chapter five king Belshazzar was weighed in the balance and found wanting. Through this year let God hold your hand and lead you. The scales will tip in your favor. Blessings for the Year…. Jim

Challenge

"State of the Union," how about "State of the Church? Ron Sider in his new book "The Scandal of the Evangelical Conscience" writes;

Scandalous behavior is rapidly destroying American Christianity! Pollsters are finding Evangelical Christians divorce their spouses just as often as their secular neighbors. They beat their wives as often as their neighbors. They are almost as materialistic as and even more racist than their pagan friends. They claim that Jesus is Lord but with their actions they demonstrate allegiance to money, sex, and self-fulfillment. My challenge this morning is to make sure our Faith is a matter of the Heart rather than an Oral Whirlwind. In John 12:26 Jesus said **"If anyone serves me let him follow me: and where I am, there my servant will be also**". That calls for Discipleship and change of lifestyle. There is no such thing as "Cheap Grace" where you just say the magic words and receive a fire insurance policy. In the New Birth our sins are surely all forgiven but unless Jesus becomes Lord and Master of our life religion is only a farce. Following Jesus is a daily walk. Let's do it! Blessings to You…Jim

David and Bathsheba

And then there was Ahithophel, a lifelong advisor to King David and now also to Absalom. The Bible says his advice was as if one had inquired at the oracle of God but for years this man held a secret unforgiving hatred in his heart toward his King. Now in 2 Samuel 17 he joins Absalom in the revolution. His goal is to become a National hero and kill his old enemy all at the same time. However the scheme backfires. After revealing his heart for all to see, his advice is not followed. He returns to set his house in order and commits suicide by hanging himself. Paul says in Ephesians 4:31 **"Let all bitterness, wrath and anger be put away from you. Be kind, tenderhearted, forgiving one another even as God in Christ forgave you**". Two words, I forgive, would have changed his life completely and preserved it in the end. Ahithopfel was the grandfather of Bathsheba. See 2 Samuel 11:3 & 23:34.....Jim Mullett

Hector

Something I seen on our recent trip to Guatemala reminds me of Jesus' prayer for his people in the Gospel of John chapter seventeen. Verses 22 and 26 read: **And the glory which You gave Me, I have given them; that they may be one, even as we are one: And I have declared to them Your name that the love with which You loved me may be in them, and I in them.** No matter what their denomination or culture, God's people become one when love becomes operative at the point of human need.

I sat at a table beside a man named Hector. His father had been physically and mentally disabled by unspeakable torture at the hand of the Guatemalan Military. At age ten Hector began life on the city dump along with 4000 other people scavenging and fighting for scraps of food to stay alive. When he was fifteen a Catholic family cleaned him up and fed him from their table however Hector wanted nothing to do with a God who favored the rich with no justice for the poor. His new family helped him continue his education and then one day he met a Protestant pastor who told him Jesus was also a poor person who died unjustly at the hand of evil people. Today Hector is very quiet and humble but he has become one with God's wonderful people through their love. Jim Mullett

Truth Comes to the Light

Jesus was very specific to Nicodemus that entering the Kingdom of God is conditional. He said unless one is born again he cannot see the Kingdom of God. He said whoever believes in Him should not perish but have everlasting life. He said he who does not believe is condemned. He said unless one is born of water and of the Spirit he cannot see the Kingdom of God. Born Again? At my invitation He enters my heart and gives His divine life to me and my spirit is made alive in Him. He concludes his discourse with Nicodemus in John 3: 21 by saying **"He who does the truth comes to the light that his deeds may be clearly seen that they have been done in God".** A born again Christian can and will be identified by his behavior. It takes more than just speaking the magic words. Jim Mullett

Out of the Abundance

Out of the abundance of the heart the mouth speaks!! Luke 6:45. This week the eyes of the whole world are on Beijing. The athlete will never win the gold unless his entire heart is in his chosen performance. The musician will not excel unless the music springs from the heart and spills over the piano keys or whatever instrument he chooses. He must love it first before the audience can appreciate and applaud. And we can never exhibit the compassion and love of Jesus unless He is first in our heart; Oh but wait! It's not that easy. Before one can receive the Olympic Gold there must first be years of grueling sacrifice and self-denial. The first time Tyler blew the trombone it drove me crazy! The disciples when first they met the Lord still wanted to call fire down on their enemies. To love as Jesus loved is too big an order to learn in a day or a year. It my even take a lifetime before we even get near that goal but the process starts now with a decision of the heart. Jesus said when you open your mouth you reveal your heart… Jim Mullett

The Greedy Little Guy

I've been watching this nasty little hummingbird that seems to have picked up some bad attitudes. There is more than enough nectar in the feeder provided by his Heavenly Father and me for all the birds in the forest. Yet this greedy little guy spends so much of his energy and time driving others away he himself hardly has time to drink. Might this be a lesson for us as we grapple with the immigration problem and spend millions building a fence around ourselves? I would remind that little bird of the words of Jesus in

Matthew 6: **Do not worry saying what shall we eat or what shall we drink or what shall we wear? For after all these things the Gentiles seek. Your Heavenly Father knows that you need all these things. But seek first the Kingdom of God and His righteousness and all these things shall be added to you**. Next time the subject comes up ask yourself if you really want to be like that little hummer…Jim Mullett

A Quiet and Humble Man

OK I confess! I was getting a bit disillusioned with the Christian Faith. It seemed more and more a Christian was only identified as being anti-abortion, anti-gay, pro-Israel, politically aligned and on the bandwagon for legalizing morality. Last evening after paying for a motel room what do I find therein but a copy of the Book of Mormon. My attitude was; well what the heck anyhow. Today I went to the funeral of my dear and longtime friend. He was a very quiet and humble man who simply went about the business of caring for and loving his wife and family and he made no distinction in his community of whom he served and loved. I was amazed not only by the number of people who packed the church but also how many gave testimony of being touched by God through the quiet witness of this faithful servant. His Motto: the words of Jesus "**Let your light so shine before men that they may glorify your Father**

in Heaven". My faith was restored. This guy was for real! ... Jim Mullett

Learning Responsibility

I had a ringside seat working the ice cream booth for the Rotarians at the fair this week. We were set up just behind the main arena where the 4-H kids proudly showed off their animals to the judges. These young folks have been learning responsibility all summer as they pampered and fed their charges under the watchful eye of their 4-H leaders and parents. This is what family and community is all about for in a few short years they themselves will be the leaders in Jackson County. Far too many men in our county have abandoned their families leaving responsibility for the kids to wives and community. There's something about the farm; it don't pay much but it builds character. Our Creator God was very wise when He instituted the family. Not Adam and Steve but Adam and Eve were His design. In Noah's ark it was a male and his female. His instruction after the flood was **"Be fruitful and multiply".** God knows the strength of the Nation is rooted in the family. 4-H is a training opportunity that should not be taken lightly. Oh! The scene of the week was a small goat, sparkling clean and dancing down the fairway slipping away from all who were trying to catch him....What a happy time! Jim Mullett

Wisdom of the Creator

One cup of sugar, three cups of warm water, a drop of red food coloring and the hummingbirds just love it. And I love just sitting and watching them swarm around the feeder. And there is the little chipmunk running to his hole with his cheeks bulging with bird seed swiped from the cardinal's supply. Mom and Pop bluebird have just completed raising their second family of the season. Even the crows come for a daily ration. All are God's little creatures and welcome in our yard but the deer get my divided affection. I love to see them roaming around but I wish they wouldn't eat my little green apples and certainly not the tender buds from Isabel's flowers! God however has a way of making things right for He said in Genesis 9:3 **every moving thing that lives (deer for example) shall be food for you!** Oh the wisdom of the Creator; without the hunter those lovely deer would become a real nuisance. Jim Mullett

Daily Bread

Give us this day our daily bread. So Jesus teaches us to pray. He had a deep concern for Hungry people as evidenced in the miraculous feeding of the five thousand and also when He broke the Sabbath rules with His disciples in the grain field. Sunday dinner is always a big family event at our house. The hungry are far from my thoughts when the platter is passed the second time. I think more about the scales. I wonder what our diet would be if Jesus filled our plate and served it to us; Oh please God, rice once a week is enough. After all, we do live in America. Last Sunday that roast was simply delicious....I wonder how far from our front door we need to go to find a hungry person? ... Jim Mullett

Water into Wine

It must have been some celebration the day Jesus turned six kegs of water into wine! At twenty to thirty gallons each that was a minimum of 120 gallons; one quart each for 480 guests. It doesn't tell us who the bride and groom were but families make memories on special occasions. This one is remembered in John chapter two. Last evening I stood at our door as Fourth of July Fireworks boomed and flashed over several miles away. I'll never forget 22 years ago on the Fourth our first grandchild was born. Three years ago all, well fifty or more of Isabel's Canadian relatives were on our front yard. The fireworks cost much more than the food but family memories and relationships created that evening are priceless and will last throughout all of our lives. Last Sunday I wrote of the poor and hungry among us. Today remember that joyous and extravagant celebrations are just as important. Both were experienced by Jesus and both are necessary for Christian people....Jim Mullett

The Minor Prophet

There is an obscure little book in the Old Testament called Nahum. It's generally overlooked, never the subject of a sermon. We call him a Minor Prophet. **He speaks of chariots raging in the streets, jostling one another in the roads and running like lightning.** Sound like a prophecy about today? Yes, but no, it is a prophecy against the city of Nineveh. One hundred years had passed since Jonah had preached there. The city turned to God and escaped destruction. Now again a new generation forgot God and was facing judgment. The grandparents somehow had failed to pass their new-found faith on to their children. So it is a lesson for us today. Let your children see the satisfaction and joy of following Jesus. If faith is genuine others will take note...... Jim Mullett

A New Body

Today we visited the cemetery where 43 years ago we buried our 3 month old son. Isabel wondered if in Heaven he would still be a baby or perhaps an adult. Well probably neither since in 1 Corinthians 15 Paul is very specific in teaching two different bodies for us. **Verse 46: First is the natural body then comes a spiritual body. Verse 36 - 38: What you sow is not made alive unless it dies then God gives it a body as He pleases. Verse 51: A mystery, we shall all be changed. Death is swallowed up in victory.**

This Memorial Day as we remember our loved ones who have gone before it's very comforting to know God's loving care for us does not end at the grave. We are his forevermore. What a great God we serve……… Jim Mullett

Please, God

It was a sad event. She was only in the early forties. They said it was cirrhosis of the liver. We knew this person when she was in eighth grade and pregnant, abused and raped by a family member who then went to prison and later died. The child went into the state foster care system and was forgotten by society. It was a tough funeral. Please, God, in your great Love and Grace, will you find a home in heaven for persons who cannot overcome the trauma of childhood abuse? You once said **"Suffer the little children to come unto me. Of such is the Kingdom Of God."** Oh and teach us to be more caring and supportive of others who are having a hard time…. Jim Mullett

Throw It Over a Bridge

So I just went to the Post Office and filed my taxes. Now to get that extra rebate our president promised and it is meant to be spent on anything I want. It's good for the economy they say. I have no pressing need for it so… shall I splurge, hoard, or as Clarence

Jordan once suggested to someone, throw it over a bridge, just get rid of it! The writer of Hebrews in chapter 12 tells us to **lay aside every weight and the sin which so easily ensnares us and let us run with endurance the race that is set before us, looking unto Jesus...** Hey, I'll bet if I prayed about it the Lord could give me a few good suggestions how best to use my "extra" money.....Jim Mullett

Like a Common Criminal

Palm Sunday; Jesus takes His famous ride into Jerusalem. The crowds shout **Hosanna to the Son of David, blessed is He who comes in the name of the Lord**! Isaiah prophesied **My glory I will not give to another. (Isaiah 42:8**) But His real Glory was a week away on a Cross. What a paradox! It was there He died like a common criminal but in his death and Resurrection He gained a victory no man in all history can match. You and I can share that victory every day as we meet the forces of evil in our world and know the devil was defeated on Mount Calvary 2000 years ago. Our sins are forgiven and we have been set free. In my heart those words still ring through the ages; Thine is the glory Risen Conquering Son! Hosanna to the Son of David! Jim Mullett

The Rose Garden

And a big Pennsylvania win this week for Hillary! I admire her fortitude and persistence. The media was saying she just as well give up and quit. But no, she has her eye on a prize and a quitter will never win the ultimate position. We who are in Christian service can find much in our world that is discouraging. Even in our churches Satan is alive and well. I just read the book of Jeremiah. He spent a lot of time in tears over the wicked conditions within his Nation. In chapter twenty he said, **"I will not make mention of Him nor speak anymore in His name but His word was in my heart like a burning fire shut up in my bones. I was weary of holding it back and I could not!"** Be it in the Oval Office or Heaven you will not slide in on a bed of roses. Oh but there is a Rose garden at the White House. In Heaven however the Roses never fade.....On Earth the Holy Spirit is a living force in the life of God's people moving us on to the next victory... Jim Mullett

In Times like These

Blessed are those who hunger and thirst for righteousness. Oh our beloved nation is in trouble. Home foreclosures are rampant. Oil has gone over one hundred dollars a barrel. Recession is staring us in the face. Greed and poverty are evident everywhere while we spend billions in Iraq. Please God, give us a candidate that will solve our problems! But wait, Jesus is the answer. He lives His divine life through His people. He instructs us to **Let your light so shine**. Don't go yelling about it, just live it. What better times then these to relax, take out the bible and once more read that great Sermon on the Mount in Matthews gospel. After all, we are the salt of the earth, are we not? Salt in times like these is a preservative. Take heart, we are in God's hands. Jim Mullett

Seek First the Kingdom

Seek ye first the Kingdom of God says Jesus in the Sermon on the Mount. These days we seem to be more involved in choosing the right candidate for our own Kingdom. At least in the world I live in I hear a lot more conversation about Hillary and Obama then Jesus but then Jesus is not running for office. He already holds the top position which is quite permanent. We as His subjects are called to serve. He tells us that even a cup of cold water given in His name will be remembered. So when my aged Mother gets quite concerned about who I'll be voting for I just lean over and fluff her pillow.... Jim Mullett

Becoming One

That they may be one even as we are one. Sounds almost like a marriage! I looked high and low for my glasses and couldn't find them. At the same time Isabel was wondering what was happening with her eyes; for some reason she couldn't see the print clearly. Together we solved both of our problems when I found my glasses on her face! Not only does Jesus pray that we are one with each other. **He Prays: I in them and you in Me**. John 17: 23 Christians share their lives three ways, with each other and with the indwelling Spirit of God. When that becomes a reality there will be harmony both in the church and in the home. It could even extend out into your world! Jim Mullett

God Transforms

Proverbs 4:23 Keep **your heart with all diligence, for out of it spring the issues of life.** These issues identify our character. By them we form relationships including our relationship with God. Envy, materialism, pride and lust come from within and block our quest for peace, happiness and contentment. Self-control, gentleness and temperance build strong relationships especially in family and social life. Valentines are sweet but it takes true love to cover a multitude of sins. Knowing God transforms the heart but then it's up to us to clean out the trash. Would it be time today for a bit of inventory???... Jim Mullett

It's Not Our Problem

Mark chapter six, a crowd of five thousand Hungry men plus women and children. Then there were twelve disciples whose message to Jesus was, **send them away, it's not our problem!**! But wait, there comes a little boy with a lunch of five small cakes and two fish and offers it all to Jesus. At least the Teacher will have some food but no one in their wildest dreams expect to be fed by the child's favor. Then the sharing begins and continues until all are filled. The miracle was in the blessing. We like the lunch are never sufficient for the task God expects from us until we are blessed by the Lord. Like Isaac blessing Jacob all that the father is and has is transferred to the son. So Jesus sends upon us His Holy Spirit and we thus are empowered to carry His message to the Hungry world. To work for Jesus we must first experience a genuine personal Pentecost. Until that happens the task is far greater then we can perform and we can only send them away. Read Acts chapter one and two....Jim Mullett

Cry Out, "God, Why'?

There's nothing pretty about stage four cancer but the horror is not so real until it hits our own family or a personal friend. Then we cry out, God Why? I just don't understand why bad things happen to the best of people! Perhaps it is the precious trial of our Faith spoken of in 1 Peter 1:7 or maybe the refining process in Malachi 3. There is the beautiful picture of the ancient refiner setting beside a pot of hot bubbling silver ore. He keeps the fire under the pot just at the right temperature to bring the dross to the surface and as it rises He scoops it off. When He looks into the pot and sees his own reflection He knows the silver is pure. The tears shed in suffering are cleansing agents in the soul. A close friend went through this most intense battle for her life and when the crisis past I heard her stand in church and say "It was the most difficult year of my life but somehow it was also the best" Only God could make that possible! This week I again saw Jesus in a cancer patient.... Jim Mullett

To the Throne

From the Manger to the Throne by way of a Cross. Isaiah said "**I saw the Lord sitting on a Throne high and lifted up**" If you want to experience Christmas to the fullest possible joy you must realize that throne is not only found in the heavens but is today in the hearts of men and women and comes there by way of His Cross. There we have been forgiven and cleansed of all our unholiness. Now Paul in 1 Corinthians 3:16 says "**You are the temple of God; the Spirit of God dwells in you**". In that Manger God was on a rescue mission to save a human race that He dearly loved. How can we even comprehend such a gift of love? How stupid it would be to fill our temple with so much of this world that there would be no room in the inn left for Jesus. He is a perfect gentleman and comes in only by your invitation. Let's get the most out of this season....Jim Mullett

Resurrection Fact

Easter morning two gals by the name of Mary came to the tomb to anoint the body of Jesus. They were met by two angels who said to them: Why seek ye the living among the dead? He is not here, but He is risen. Remember how he spoke to you while he was yet in Galilee, saying the Son of man must be delivered unto the hands of sinful men and be crucified and the third day rise again. ...And they remembered.... You can read the story in Luke's gospel, chapter 24.

The resurrection is a hard fact for scientific minded people to believe. But think about this question today: How much would God be worth to you if He could not do it?? To be the God who created the universe and you and me in it, his power must be unlimited. To think that all this happened by random chance is even more ridicules then resurrection. Jim Mullett

Wrong Picture

Something seems wrong with this picture. As reported this week on NBC nightly news a Mexican man crossed our border illegally. His first action in this Country was to save the life of a six year old orphan found wondering in the desert and taking him to the border authorities. He was then arrested and returned to Mexico. Like it or not this was the exact opposite of Paul's instruction to Christians in Romans 12. "**Have regard for good things in the sight of all men. Overcome evil with good".** It seems the majority of professing Christians in the USA would support deportation without regard to the individual person. Would it not have been more honorable if we had rewarded this man with a good job in return for a life saved? It seems we have our Faith in one box and our Nationality in another. To follow Jesus our words and deeds must be integrated. I find this to be an everyday challenge. How about you? …….Jim Mullett

Before they call

This week I'm asking all of us to pray for two servants of God who are suffering. First a friend offers this request for her pastor, who three months ago had both knees replaced. Due to MRSA infections nothing is healing and he is faced with going through the same ordeal again. Second is a personal friend in Arcadia, FL. Who has bravely fought a long battle with Leukemia and the past two weeks underwent surgery on both eyes for glaucoma. Hey wait; I got to rewrite this as a praise report! I just received an update from both of these persons. God had touched them both! Bruce has finally responded to the antibiotics and Ken can see clearly. I need to change my scripture from Isaiah 43:2. Now it is Isaiah 65: 24.

Before they call, I will answer and while they are still speaking I will hear. How amazing is our God! Jim Mullett

Selfish Ambition

Correction: Ken had surgery, not for glaucoma as reported last Sunday but it was for cataracts. Sorry Ken, my mistake. Therefore today an appropriate topic might be on humility. We might take the example from Jesus our leader. Philippians chapter two: **He took the form of a servant and coming in the likeness of men; He humbled himself and became obedient to the point of death, even the death of the Cross.** He invites us to a choice of bearing the cross with him, dying to selfish ambitions, totally empty with nothing of value to offer God or man. It was at that point that God highly exalted his Son Jesus and it is there that Jesus becomes visible in us. He shines forth in all His glory. This kind of death does not come easy or in one experience or in one day. It's a continual struggle. The "old man" in us does not want to stay dead. Nor can we raise ourselves to New Life. It is a work of God. Just trust Him… Jim Mullett

Ultimate Destruction

Oh that lonely and bored Maytag Repairman! This week I needed to give him a service call. I tried to fix the washer myself but ran into the need of special tools; I needed help to finish the job. The only alternative was to throw away a good washer and buy a new one. Life is like that especially for us self-sufficient macho men. We like to steer our own ship but when we get lost there is a Higher Power that we must call on to get direction, sometimes even to be carried back on track. Refusing God in our life only leads to ultimate destruction. This week let's remember Psalms 121**: I will lift up my eyes to the hills from whence comes my help. My help comes from the Lord who made heaven and earth**. Oh Goody, the Maytag man even needed to borrow one of my tools! What does God need from you this week? What do you need from God? ..... Jim Mullett

PS: Just a health update: its Saturday 5:00 PM and I just returned from a somewhat unexpected stay in Riverside Hospital in Columbus. Diagnosis was a 100% heart block between the upper & lower chambers. Electrically they just weren't speaking to each other. So I have a new pacemaker. Hope to have an "all clear" within a few weeks....JM

Ugly Mess

When life hands you a lemon you can experience a very bitter taste or you can make sweet lemonade. This week a friend reminded me that adversity can be a positive factor in who we are but it takes patience. The trial of faith is a refining fire built under us by the Holy Spirit. When we are angry the dross comes to the surface for all to see. It is then that we pray, Oh God help me clear away this ugly mess! In Psalms 51 David prayed, **Create in me a clean heart Oh God and renew a steadfast spirit in me.** How sweet it is to look your adversary in the eye and win, not by violence or retaliation but by the way of love that Jesus taught. It was a lesson I had to learn... Life is not always fair... Jim Mullett

Concealed Identity

The status of Jewish women in Hebrew culture was extremely inferior to that of men. They were excluded from public life. Outside they were required to cover themselves with two head veils to conceal their identity. She was to remain unseen. She could be divorced for talking to someone on the street. She was forbidden to teach or to study the Torah. She was confined to domestic chores and a slave to her husband. The husband alone had the right to divorce his wife. Not much different from the plight of many women in Eastern culture today. Paul instructs women to keep these social customs: cover your head, be quiet in church, if you want to know anything ask your husband at home. However Jesus didn't hesitate to violate social norms and elevate women to a new dignity and status. Luke 10: 38 – 42 is a good example. Martha is in the kitchen doing what "good girls" are supposed to do, serving men. Her sister Mary is totally out of order having a religious discussion with Jesus and Martha complains but Jesus gave Mary the right to choose and said, "**Mary has chosen that good part which will not be taken away from her**. Paul also recognized that in Christ there is no gender difference, Galatians 3:28. I like what Jesus did for the gals…Jim Mullett

Draw a Line

Where do you draw the line? This was a question recently ask of me. The implication was that the church needs to draw a line in the sand which its members may not cross. Jesus drew such a line when he said, "**You are forgiven, now go and sin no more**". He also drew a line when He said "**Judge not, that you be not judged**". In God's Kingdom God alone maintains the right to judge human behavior. The scriptures are also clear on what God expects of His subjects. So where does this leave the church? Paul instructs the Corinthian church to expel persons who live in open defiance of God's Law but it is never the duty of the church to define what constitutes sin; the scriptures do that and we are to uphold it. In Jewish times the "Tradition of the Elders" also known as the Mishnah went beyond the Law of Moses to spell out the dos' and don'ts of Jewish religion. Jesus deliberately broke many of their rules. I suspect there are rules in our churches today that He would also ignore. Rules are necessary for children but for the truly mature Christian God writes his laws on our heart and we live from the inside out….Jim Mullett

Senior Years

So what do retired people do besides go to Florida in the winter? Well, like today a group of us got together to renew old acquaintance and remember all the good times of days of yore. There were lots of eyeglasses, hearing aids, a cane or two, false teeth and artificial joints and truth are told probably a few pacemakers. It's the Golden Years! It would really be sad if all we had to remember was our passing power, fame and wealth. Solomon in Ecclesiastes advises: **Remember now your Creator in the days of your youth.** Letting the Creator control all of life makes the ageing process the best, the richest and most happy time of all. To age gracefully also involves giving up control of our physical care and material goods to other people with whom we have developed loving relationships. Do it now while your Creator still grants you the good sense to do it right. The Golden Years are like a game between the individual and the health professional. The contest is who will own your gold after you die! Quite a challenge for us.....Jim Mullett

Walking the Pathway

High stakes gambling is not only happening in Las Vegas. It is most prevalent in the valley of the shadow of death where folks are betting their eternal soul that they have one more day to get right with God. We are all walking that pathway of life that will ultimately lead to our demise. We can walk in peace and confident assurance; I will fear no evil for God is with me. He leads me beside still waters. He feeds me in green pastures. He restores my soul. Even occasional discipline with the rod and staff is a blessing for it keeps me from straying away and getting lost. Surely goodness and mercy will follow me every day of my life as I walk that valley. Psalms 23 is so beautiful yet people will go on gambling.....Jim Mullett

Size of Eggs

I was fixing a small snack and set two cartons of eggs on the counter. Immediately I noticed one dozen was much smaller than the other although both were sold as grade A large. I got out my scale and discovered a twenty five percent variance. So who sets the standard for the size of eggs? How about a standard for Christians! On CNN Thursday night, "God's Christian Warriors" there were a host of pastors setting a political agenda for us to live by. However there was one pastor who dared preach a message on Jesus' instruction to love our enemies. He was branded as Un-American and lost 1000 members. Thankfully he gained 1000 others who were ready to live by the message of Jesus. President Carter noted that mixing politics and religion is detrimental to both the Church and State. Our involvement in Iraq seems to prove his point. Jesus never attempted to use legal means to enforce His teachings, not from the Sanhedrin or the Roman government and nether should we. He writes his laws on our heart. That's our standard! Oh by the way...The large eggs were sold by the Kroger Company....Jim Mullett

Important Enough

Hey wait; this afternoon is our annual business meeting at Church. Not a fun time but the Pot Luck meal sounds good. If I had been on the ball with our travel schedule I could have missed all this but no; our church is important enough to me to make this meeting a top priority. This is our home church. My children and grandchildren are involved in it and I want it to be here for them after I am in Heaven. Here they learned a way of peace that our society desperately needs to experience. Here is where they were taught morals and values that kept them from the addictions of many of their peers. It wasn't easy for our High School age daughter on New Year Eve to get out of the car and walk home when her two best friends pulled out a bottle of booze. Church is hard work but it sure can pay big dividends for a family and you can be sure I'll be there this afternoon with my two cents worth of wisdom and one sure vote! It's for the next generation..... Jim

The House on Wall Street

Two men built a house: one on a solid foundation, the other on the sand and you know the rest of the story in Matthew seven. Not only Wall Street but also many on Main Street built their wealth by greed and on credit but without enough collateral. This week the rain came in a deluge and the house tumbled. Jesus however was not talking about financial markets. In the previous chapters He lays out a solid foundation for happy and successful living. Blessed are the meek. Marriage is a sacred union. Be as good as your word and love your enemies. Be generous with your charitable deeds and here is a model prayer you can use: Seek the Kingdom of God and you won't need to worry about tomorrow. Hey if you can't sleep because of our broken economy get up and read the Sermon on the Mount. Next week I have invited Dorothy Tress Anderson of Okeechobee, Florida to write about "Joy in the morning"…Jim

Sing Praise to the Lord

Psalm 30:4-5

Sing praises to the Lord, you Saints of His, and give thanks at the remembrance of His holy name. For His anger is but for a moment, His favor is for life; weeping may endure for a night, but joy comes in the morning.

Have you ever noticed that some Christians seem to be happy all the time? It seems as though they never grieve. The truth is, though, that no one is happy all the time. Part of being in a world of sin is a life filled with emotional upset, enemies, sorrow, retaliations, bitterness, sadness, gossip, physical pain, death of children, spouses, parents of young children…and the list goes on.

The difference for the Christian is awareness, in the middle of all these difficulties of life that our God will always take care of us. Even though our life may be filled with all kinds of trials and burdens, we know that weeping may endure for a night, but JOY COMES IN THE MORNING.

Written by Dorothy Tress Anderson

The Worst of Lies

The most devastating lie in all history was told to Eve by Satan back in the Garden of Eden; you can replace God and be First Lady of Creation! Today it's called "humanism" and people are still believing and doing it. Paul in Romans chapter one addresses the problem; **Professing to be wise, they became fools. They exchanged the truth of God for the lie and worshiped and served the Creature rather than the Creator. For this reason God gave them up to vile passions.** He then lists a catalog of sins that makes one shudder. How much happier our life will be if we give God his rightful place and worship only Him. He then produces in us the Fruit of the Spirit as listed in Galatians 5:22 & 23 **Love, Joy, Peace, longsuffering, kindness, goodness, faithfulness, gentleness and self-control**. God's Kingdom is kind of up-side-down when compared to our present social order of things.... Blessing to you today...Jim Mullett

The Outstretched Hand

One of the more difficult sermons I have tried to preach was when my right arm was in a sling. I don't remember the subject at all that morning but I found speaking without gestures most difficult. The body speaks louder than the voice and often more honestly. The outstretched hand with the palm up means I need something from you or I have something to offer you. The raised hand with palm out means I surrender to you. The next time you pray try doing it with only your hands and ears. Let your voice be silent. Stand before Jesus and use one of these gestures and then close your eyes and listen to what Jesus would say to you. Offer your heart, surrender your will and receive His gifts. Wow! I'm getting blessed just thinking about it. Jim Mullett

Fundamental Ways

Oh the quest for power and control! It drives our political candidates. In business it makes one rich. It drives good people to corruption and even creeps into the Christian Community where Jesus

Christ is the professed Lord and Master. In my last Newsweek magazine someone wrote, "The Major Religions are alike in fundamental ways: Their founders tried to teach the same universal values and their teachings are for the most part universally ignored. Despite their entreating us to treat each other with love, kindness and respect, mans' inhumanity to man rages on". How we react when our own **Seat of Power** is threatened says much about who we really are in the core of our being. Jesus taught His Disciples: **It shall not be so among you; but whoever desires to become great among you shall be your servant, even the Son of Man did not come to be served but to serve and give his life a ransom for many. Mark 10: 35 – 45** Happiness is not found in power……Blessings…Jim Mullett

In God We Trust

The new dollar coin is making somewhat of a sensation among Christians. There is even a call for a boycott. In God We Trust seems to be missing along with the date, the mint mark and E Pluribus Unum, all gone! But wait! It's all there! It's just been moved to a place where we don't expect to find it. In todays' world of technology change happens so fast I find it hard to keep up. Just give me a phone with ten numerals; one that works when I need it. God is like that, constant, unmoved, always there. David said **if I take the wings of the morning and dwell in the uttermost parts of the**

sea even there your hand shall lead me; Psalms 139. Even if they would take the inscription from my coins it would not change God one bit. Sure I appreciate the inscription but He does not need me to come to His defense...Have a good week...Jim Mullett

Independence Day

BOOM BANG FIREWORKS FREEDOM!!! The cost is far greater than the price of the fireworks; Young men and women coming home leaving behind their limbs and souls, too many returning in body bags. Until it becomes me or my soldier I cannot fully comprehend the true cost. To compensate the soldier we give them the highest honor while our large corporations make enormous profits and we all become rich. Six hundred dollars for this new gismo called an I-phone?? There has got to be a better way and I believe Jesus offers it when He said "**If the Son will set you free you will be free indeed**". True freedom does not need to hide in fear behind walls, fences and homeland security. It has nothing to do with wealth or fame. Until we as a Nation and its people are willing to trust in Jesus who we call the Prince of Peace and learn from Him how to live in peace our youth in their prime of life will continue to be blown apart. Read it in John 8: 31-36 and at least think about it. Blessings to you today...Jim

Resolutions

A popular New Year resolution is to diet and lose weight. Oh yes me too, at least so said my doctor! Hunger and homelessness in America is forcing its way into our consciousness with the housing crunch. Easy credit and no money down made it possible to live above our means. To those of us who knew the value of savings accounts it's easy to look the other way and blame the poor for their own mistakes. It's difficult for me to subsidize the cost of addictions such as drugs alcohol and tobacco. As rich Christians we need to find a balance between holding others responsible for their plight and offering a loving hand up from the pits. Jesus said **the poor will always be with us**. Some of them need our example and counsel. All need our love...... Jim Mullett

Lucky Spider

Yesterday I watched a small spider walk across my carpet. My impulse was to step on it but my foot was too slow in responding to the brain. Later while contemplating that tiny bit of biological life I marveled at a God who created such a bug that could run away to safety on such spindly little legs. How limited was that spider's comprehension of a life as big as me. Could it even compare to my limited comprehension of the Eternal God? Yet God takes notice of you and I and spared our life so that we could live in His house. He endued us with his own spiritual life so we could know Him and have fellowship with Him. He put us in charge of His whole wonderful Creation. I take you to Psalms 8: **What is man that you are mindful of him? You made him a little lower than the angels and crowned him with glory and honor. You have made him to have dominion over the works of your hand.** So why did I want to kill that little spider anyhow? Jim

<u>Fellow Traveler</u>

What a true fable! There's this duck and a frog both sharing the same pond. But the pond dries up so neither can survive without water. No problem for the duck as he can just fly to the next pond. The frog bites onto the duck's tail and both are on the way when a fellow traveler comments; what a grand idea, who thought of that? The frog immediately opens his mouth to take credit and plunges to his death. Jesus said in the Sermon on the Mount, **Take heed that you do not do your charitable deeds before men to be seen by them. Otherwise you have no reward from your Father in heaven.** I often remember Isabel's comment; it's amazing what can be accomplished when you don't care who gets the credit. Try it this week just once. It's a great feeling… Oh, I won't sign my name to this one!

The Family of God

At our church we often sing "I'm So Glad I'm a Part of The Family of God". On the other side of that coin are broken and shattered homes where kids are caught in the turmoil of wickedness and sin. Last Sunday I had the joy of baptizing into our family at Hillside a lovely young lady who at the age of twelve was struggling for a better life. This week she and her younger brother are thrust into the child foster care system. Today I vividly remember the words of Jesus when He said **"Suffer the little children to come unto me for of such is the Kingdom Of God".** Pray with us this week for Jessica and Billy. Pray for the Family of God that we may be patient and confident in God's Grace that is greater than all the sins these two children are called upon to endure. And thank Him for Christian Parents who loved us and gave us a safe and loving childhood. No, life is not always fair but what a difference a solid Faith in God can make…… Jim Mullett

A Touch of God

And then there was Jacob. He was raised in a Godly home but his Grandpa and Dad both lied when convenient. Mom was a bit deceitful to Dad. Esau never did become religious and Jacob was a schemer. Oh yes he met God in a very dramatic way at Bethel but it didn't change him a bit. For the next twenty one years he scammed from uncle Laban most of his possessions. Finally one dark night the chips were down and he wrestled with God. When morning came Jacob was a changed man. Now in Genesis 47 he is an old man carried by his famous son into the presence of Pharaoh and there he pronounces a blessing on this greatest Head of State. How different it was from the blessing he had received from Isaac years before. Family status and possessions were long forgotten. This blessing to Pharaoh was a touch of God. Are we in position to so touch our neighbors? … Jim Mullett

On Our Most Hot-button Issue

Change is coming to Washington. We also need change in the Religious Right. Our efforts to overthrow Roe v Wade have been counterproductive, here's why:

First, we have become a major voting block for the Republican Party. They know as soon as they give us what we want the focal point that has held us together will be lost. We would disintegrate and they would lose our strength at the polls. That's politics pure and simple.

Second, the function of the Supreme Court is not to vote on matters of conscience. It is there solely to interpret the Constitution of the United States. Presidents and legislators know the Court may not become biased; therefore there must be a balance between liberal and conservative Judges. We have looked to the power of the State to make abortion illegal.

We must now look to the power of God in us to make it unnecessary. Let us recognize that the problem is not in Washington but in the heart and soul of our communities, our churches and in ourselves. Jesus was a servant leader. He did not use force but invited people to follow. He asks the same of us when He said "**let you light so shine before men that they may see your good works and glorify your Father in Heaven".**

Am I suggesting that we throw in the towel and quit? Absolutely not! I am suggesting that we will be more effective if we would learn to lead and leave the results to God. Jesus never looked to government or even to the Synagogue to enforce morality. We might even have some things we need to repent of....Jim Mullett

<u>The Richest Man</u>

Who Wants To Be A Millionaire? Today it can be you. Your scripture is Romans 11:33. **"Oh the depth of the riches both of the wisdom and knowledge of God! How unsearchable are his judgments and His ways past finding out".** Pick a wild flower beside the path, smell the fragrance and study its beauty. Spend some one on one time with a small child. Give and receive a smile from someone you have chosen to love. When you go to bed tonight think of the day and count your blessings. You will know what a millionaire really is because it could be you.

Jim Mullett

The Beginning and the End

Sunday Morning Inspiration

November 16, 2008

We are all on a journey traveling the road of life. I am looking at the first "Inspiration" I wrote on April 9, 2000. My purpose has been to be not only inspirational but also to be provocative, causing both you and I to think and know where we stand in Christ and hopefully take that next step toward home. I deeply appreciate all of you who have responded to me with your comments and questions and also with your challenges.

Ronald Sider reflects my concern for Christian America in his book, "The Scandal of the Evangelical Conscience"; why are Christians living just Like the Rest of The World? When I read it I become aware of my own hypocrisy. Then I read my favorite psychologist Dr. M. Scott Peck and his book "Further Along The Road Less Traveled", The Unending Journey Toward Spiritual Growth. Now I know I may not judge another for we are all at a different position on that road.

After eight years as I close out this chapter of Sunday Morning Inspiration I leave you with my first lines:

Sunday Morning Inspiration

April 9, 2000

I am lonely. There is no one else like me in this whole wide world. This "I-entity" that is me is different from each and every other person that ever lived. We are all unique people. Our separate personalities and physical features, like fingerprints, make all of us identifiable one from another. God loves variety and he loves you and me just as we are. Today's scripture is found in the Living Bible, 1 John 3:1, **"See how very much our Heavenly Father loves us, for he allows us to be called his children**. – Think of it—and we really are." Remember today how special you are! Jim Mullett

Epilogue

Throughout these writings, I have emphasized my understanding of the New Testament Jesus and His teaching concerning the use of force and violence in human relations, including military service. One scripture however that I have struggled with is Luke 22:36 where Jesus clearly instructs His disciples: He who has no sword let him sell his garment and buy one.

After spending His entire ministry teaching a message of love, now, at the very end when the chips are down, why would He negate what He has stood for and previously taught? Do we perhaps in our Western technological culture have difficulty understanding a more primitive way of life two thousand years ago, or even in less developed countries today?

That day Peter certainly understood that sword as a weapon even though Jesus said two swords are enough; two swords for thirteen men being attacked by a hundred Roman soldiers? But then, Peter knew his leader. For three years he followed a miracle working Jesus, feeding the crowd of five thousand with a lad's lunch, healing the sick and raising the dead, walking on water, even controlling the weather. Surely a Roman garrison would not present a problem.

Tonight's the time for the deliverance of his beloved Jewish nation from the domination of Rome! Tomorrow his Messiah would sit on the Throne of David. It was no idle talk when Peter declared his allegiance and willingness to die for the cause. After-all, had not Gideon routed the entire Midianite army with no sword at all?

How disappointed and disillusioned he must have been when Jesus stopped him from the attack on Malchus that night in the garden and then to see Him arrested and carried away to judgment, his lifelong dream of freedom was shattered. So many bands of his countrymen in previous years had died in the attempt to overthrow the enemy. Now the very one that could do it, the one to whom he had given his loyalty and support is ready to give it up without a fight!

How angry he must have been standing outside in the courtyard cursing and denying that he ever knew the man. But we still must deal with the paradox of Jesus' words on this last day of ministry to His disciples.

Previously I referred to Dr. Scott Peck and his tools of discipline, the fourth one being finding a balance, flexibility in our understanding of rules and issues in daily living. A rule that can't be bent may at times become a curse instead of a blessing.

Somewhere in the middle of this theological debate I find Jesus holding a Roman coin and declaring, Render to Caesar the things that are Caesar's and to God the things that are God's. It is in this declaration that we find a balance in the teaching of our Lord, an obligation to government as well as to God.

God however must be the Supreme Ruler of our life. We must never follow the dictates of an evil despot when they are in conflict with the rule of God. In our democracy, we the people and government set the laws designed for the safety and wellbeing of our citizens.

When those laws are violated, whether it's against our neighbor or against us personally, it becomes our duty to bring the perpetrator to justice even if it involves removing him from society. Thus we "render to Caesar". When a law is in conflict with the teaching of Jesus, we "render to God".

If I were on the military, I'd make a commitment to follow every order of my commanding officer. Therein I have a problem, for there is a higher authority to which I have voluntarily committed my life. This creates a constant tension between conscience and nationalism.

What shall we do about the Hitlers of this world? I do applaud our President for the way the Navy Seals took out Bin Laden and for the recent rescue in Somalia. I must also admire Dr. Martin Luther King for taking a non-violent stand against the evils of racism and segregation when he knew it would cost him his life.

It was not until I took a vacation to Jamaica that I finally came to an understanding of Jesus' words in Luke 22. Many Jamaican men

I saw were carrying machetes sharp enough and big enough to take off the head of any aggressor in an instant!

What were they using them for? To whack off the end of a coconut when they were hungry or thirsty. They'd used it in the garden to cultivate around a pineapple and dig out the weeds. The morning I left I seen six men cutting the lawn at their church with their "swords". They told me they couldn't afford a luxury like a lawn mower.

It was then that the lights came on in my mind. I could only see a sword through Western eyes as a weapon of war. Jesus associated the sword with the knapsack, the money bag and the sandals. Sometimes pastors and disciples need to provide their own living. Every farmer needs a hoe, and the hunter needs a knife. Times were changing. The disciples were entering a hostile world. Two thousand years later, the teachings of Jesus are still relevant for us.

Love is stronger than the sword.
–Pastor Jim

About the authors'

Pastor Cory P. Pariseau

is the Pastor and Founder of Crossroads World Christian Center Church in Columbus, Ohio, whose mission is to reach out, through the grace of God, to those that have come to a crossroads in their lives and don't know which direction to turn. Crossroads WCCC, Pastor Pariseau and church members are touching lives and hearts in the Columbus, Ohio community and around the world daily by fulfilling The Great Commission given to all by our Lord and Savior, Jesus Christ, through the many ministries and outreaches that God's amazing power has blessed the Church with the resources to provide.

As C.E.O. and Founder of Crossroads World Christian Center Church - and many other ministries, such as The Crossroads Fellowship Tour, Crossroads Community Services and Parenting Pathways to name a few (some others are listed below) - and as both a child and a parent who's been through the Children's Services system, Pastor Pariseau knows the trials and pains of going through the system from both aspects.

For much of his life he had been in the system one way or another.

As a young child, Cory went into the foster care system when he was 4 years old. A dozen foster homes and two children's homes later, he was finally adopted at the age of 7. By the time he was 29 he had 3 children of his own and through some bad choices he made (and in an ironic twist of fate), he lost the kids to Children's Services...this after losing his marriage, his job, and everything he had worked for all his life to that point.

Pastor Cory found himself in a mental institution for 6 weeks and God came into his life and allowed him start on the journey of faith and in getting his family back. In July 2001, the kids came back to stay with Pastor Pariseau for good. It was a hard and confusing journey. With everything he went through, he did find a system of support for single parents, but he often thought that a system of support, giving back and sharing with those other families who were going down the same path (of being involved with Children's Services) would have been a true blessing to him. Thus, Parenting Pathways, and many other helping ministries were born through the years.

Pastor Cory has also been a loyal employee of Wal-Mart Distribution Center in Grove City, Ohio for 15 years.

- **2002**: Cory joined a Parents Anonymous group that helped him through raising his 3 children, where he quickly became a Parent leader in the group and spoke to countless Parent classes about Parent Leadership • **2002-2008**: Cory worked with Catholic Social Services of Central Ohio talking to their Parent World classes
- **2003-2006**: Cory was asked to be on the National Parent Leadership Team of Parents Anonymous, participating and helping with the Best Practices for Parent Leaders sessions, as well as talking to Congressional leaders on Parent Leadership
- **2003-2006**: Cory helped with the National Training Institute for Parents Anonymous in Washington D.C.
- **2003-2005**: Cory helped with the National Training Institute for Parents Anonymous in San Diego, California
- **2005**: Pastor Cory was given the CAVA Award by Franklin County Children's Services for advocating parent leadership in the community
- **2005**: Pastor Cory founded Crossroads World Christian Center Church in Columbus, Ohio
- **2005**: Pastor Cory founded Parenting Pathways in Columbus, Ohio
- **2006**: Pastor Cory was presented with the Jolly K Award for the State of Ohio
- **2006-2008**: Pastor Cory sat on the Board of Regents of Crossroads Christian College and Seminary in Florida

- **2007**: Pastor Cory founded Country Hands helping inner-city youth experience a change in environment
- **2007**: Cory sat on a panel at the Ohio Foster Parents Conference
- **2007-2008**: Cory sat on the committee with Buckeyes Boys Ranch with Birth Parent Incentive
- **2007**: Cory joined Children's Hospitals Inter-Faith Network to confront abuse in our community
- **2008**: Pastor Cory was ask to set on the committee for a Day of Hope, a community event day celebrating drug and alcohol abuse recovery
- **2009**: Pastor Cory Found and started Crossroads Community Services to help offer and link services to the community of Central, Ohio
- **2010**: Cory started Crossroads World Christian Center Online Community Church
- **2011**: Pastor Cory founded Crossroads World Wide Bible Institute online

Pastor Jim Mullett

Jim was born as Samuel Mullett in the State of New York soon thereafter being given the name James and finally being known as simply "Jim". In 1953 the family moved to a farm in Greenwood, Delaware. There Jim attended the Greenwood Mennonite Parochial School through grade ten. In his later teen years he enrolled in a privately sponsored Bible Institute in Kitchener, Ontario where he met and married Isabel Steckly.

After marriage the new couple moved to Southern Ohio where Jim attended Rio Grande University where he studied Creative Writing, Public Speaking and his most stimulating subject, Philosophy 104.

Today he resides along a Country highway in Jackson County, Ohio with his bride of 51 years, two children, four grandkids and five Hispanics who have become a part of the extended family.

Books Coming Soon

40 days of Cause and Affect

What you do today will affect somebody's tomorrow

All In the Family *An adoption of multicultural Family*

Speak Life *Change your atmosphere, Change the World*

Training up! *Multicultural Children*

Missing Potholes *Marriage second time around*

Information

HILLSIDE CHAPEL

1751 STATE ROUTE 788

JACKSON, OH, 45640

(740) 286-9989

http://www.thehillsidechapel.org/

Crossroads

World Christian Center Church

Pastor Cory P. Pariseau
P.O. Box 11637
Columbus, Ohio 43211
Local Phone: (614) 375-3080
Toll Free Phone: (888) 383-4321
Fax: (614) 343-9177
Email: comments@CrossroadsWCC.org
www.crossroadswcc.org

CROSS LIGHT
PUBLISHING

Cross Light Publishing is an outreach ministry of Crossroads World Christian Center Church where we publish our printed media materials, such as the CrossNEWS Newsletter, the Parenting Pathways Newsletter and books, such as *Standing at a Crossroads*, *40 Days of Cause and Affect* and *We Are All in God's Family.*

CrossPRAYER
Put the power of Prayer to work in your life! Post your prayer requests and/or become part of our Prayer Team today!
Prayer Requests

Crossroads Community Services
- *NEW SERVICES Now Available!*

Helping the community by serving others. Crossroads Community Services serves the Columbus, Ohio community in many new ways. This ministry serves to integrate many of our currently existing outreaches under one roof, such as the food pantry and providing clothing and donations of other gently used household goods and to needy central Ohio families. Donations of these things are needed and welcomed! We've recently added many additional services! Visit the Crossroads Community Services page for more information.

Crossroads World Wide Bible Institute
Each course is set up and designed to equip students for personal study of the Word of God after the conclusion of Institute training. Students learn how to study the Bible by book, chapter, paragraph, verse, and word. Other methods taught include biographical, devotional, theological, typological, and topical. Special guidelines for studying Bible poetry and prophecy are presented and students are taught methods of charting and outlining. www.crossroadswwbi.org

Parenting Pathways

The mission of this ministry is is to empower, strengthen, and lead parents who are struggling with reunification with their children through the child protective agencies and to assist all parents who are in need of support. Parenting Pathways new site is now up and running! Visit www.ParentingPathways.org to find out more.

Speak Life TV

Live in the Central Ohio area? If so, you may soon be able to view our new media outreach ministry, ***Speak Life TV*** on a local television channel. Stay tuned for more on *Speak Life TV*! www.speaklifetv.org

www.ingramcontent.com/pod-product-compliance
Ingram Content Group UK Ltd.
Pitfield, Milton Keynes, MK11 3LW, UK
UKHW040155091026
15587UKWH00018B/319

9 781619 969810